This book is to be returned on or before
the last date stamped below.

- 8 JUL 2010   2 9 JUN 2015

Stuffed Vine leaves
saved my life

WITHDRAWN

NADIA SAWALHA

*Stuffed Vine leaves
saved my life*

Doubleday

LONDON · TORONTO · SYDNEY · AUCKLAND · JOHANNESBURG

Transworld Publishers
61–63 Uxbridge Road, London W5 5SA
A Random House Group Company
www.rbooks.co.uk

First published in Great Britain
in 2010 by Doubleday
an imprint of Transworld Publishers

A CIP catalogue record for this book
is available from the British Library.

ISBN 9780385616935

Addresses for Random House Group Ltd companies outside the UK can be found at:
www.randomhouse.co.uk
The Random House Group Ltd Reg. No. 954009

The Random House Group Limited supports the Forest Stewardship Council (FSC),
the leading international forest-certification organization. All our titles that are
printed on Greenpeace-approved FSC-certified paper carry the FSC logo. Our
paper procurement policy can be found at www.rbooks.co.uk/environment

Typeset in Mrs Eaves and Akzidenz Grotesk
Printed and bound in Germany by APPL

Food photography: Steve Lee
Text design and art direction: Smith & Gilmour
Food stylist: Clare Greenstreet
Prop stylist: Liz Belton

2 4 6 8 10 9 7 5 3 1

Contents

For Mark, Maddie and Kiki Bee x

Introduction

Winning *Celebrity MasterChef* has quite simply transformed my life.
I'm sitting here in my kitchen, my girls chirping in the background,
writing my very own cookbook, having been given the opportunity
to feed more people than I ever thought possible – and I'm loving
every minute of it!

How did this happen? How have I arrived here, at my kitchen
table, not knowing how to use a laptop, typing with one finger, just
about to spill the beans (almost literally) on my family life through
the food we've cooked and eaten over the years?

Well, I've always loved food and I've always loved cooking, and yet it
took winning the coveted title of *Celebrity MasterChef* to give me a much-
needed wake-up call. When I appeared on the show I didn't think
about the fact that it was actually a television programme; I forgot that
I was taking part in something that would eventually be broadcast to
nearly 5 million people! As my family will testify, every night I would
come home maniacally driven to practise recipes, not once, but twice,
three times ... fearful of losing, worried sick about getting this or that
wrong. I was a bag of nerves, and yet it was nothing to do with being
in front of a TV audience. Indeed, it was only when I came face to face
with the judges and, for the first time, actually saw the TV cameras,
that I was painfully reminded of what I'd let myself in for ...

What drove me to a place of extreme fear, profound excitement
and, most surprisingly, unlocked in me a competitive gene I never
thought I had, was the fact that cooking lovely food really, *really*
matters to me. Not simply in an 'I must be better than everyone else'
or an 'Oh God, I mustn't look like a fool' sort of way. No. For me,
taking part in (and eventually winning) *Celebrity MasterChef* made me
fully realize that creating beautiful meals for people I care about
is one of the most important parts of who I am. For me, to cook
someone a meal is truly to give him or her something of *me*. In the
same way that writers write books and actors perform, the act of
cooking in my kitchen is an expression of my feelings and my mood.
Appearing in that gladiatorial show unlocked something in me that

had always been there but had never been given the oxygen to run riot. To quote a very famous advert, when I was told I had won I felt as though I had finally got an 'ology'. For the first time in my life, I felt qualified. It really was quite an emotional and life-affirming moment.

So it is with amazement and gratitude that I sit here now, entertaining the possibility of being able to share my innermost family foodie secrets with you.

My passion for all things foodie began a long time ago. Being brought up in an Anglo-Arab home taught me, from an early age, the importance of feeding your family fabulous food. The mantra was always, 'Good food, cooked with love, feeds the soul as well as the body.'

Let me conjure up a childhood scene ...

At weekends we would invariably have huge family gatherings. From the upstairs window my sisters and I would be looking down, watching the kasbah come to life, eager to see what our various uncles, aunties and cousins were bringing for the dinner table. Each of us three girls – Dina, Julia and I – would be salivating with nervous excitement, hoping, wishing, pleading for all our favourite dishes. Mine was always my Auntie Jamileh's meat pizzas; Julia (the youngest) usually had her hopes pinned on mussakhan, a delicious dish of roasted chicken, onion and spices; whilst Dina (the eldest) couldn't wait to thrust her left hand deep into the mansaf, a celebratory meat and yogurt dish.

From our vantage point, we'd stare wide-eyed as Auntie Jamileh led the tribe, holding aloft her show-off dish of the day – generally a battered old pressure cooker filled to the brim with all manner of vegetables stuffed with aromatic rice, lamb and nuts. Close behind her would be my cousin Laurice, giggling loudly as she teetered down the path holding a tray of home-made, sticky Arabic sweets firmly in her hands. And, more often than not, bringing up the rear would be Cousin Nayef, leaping about like a demented acrobat, somehow managing to balance an enormous bowl of painstakingly made, emerald-green tabbouleh under each arm.

Once everyone was in, the three of us would then, and only then, charge down the stairs, eager to be part of the hubbub, bit-players in the culinary show. This was always a truly magical moment in my childhood, almost as if with every step we took down the stairs we left behind our ordinary bedroom in South-east London, arriving – *bang* – in an Aladdin's cave of noise, gossip, scents, colours and flavours.

Faces would grimace and smile, dishes would be passed to and fro, floating above our heads on a sea of outstretched hands and arms, until the contents needed replenishing. Laughter would melt into shrieks, shock would be met with outrage, and my sisters and I would dart around, nibbling a bit of this, nicking a bit of that (maybe dipping into my uncle's perfect hummus), all the while keeping a keen and eager eye on the mounds of warm, syrupy pastries ...

Emotions, tastes, moods, relationships, aromas – in my rather wonderful family, *all* are totally blended. Indeed, so extreme was (and is) my family's obsession with food, that many important relationships have been forged and split asunder over things as simple as which way a vegetable has been stuffed ... or *should* have been stuffed. For us, the philosophy of food is quite simply a philosophy of life, and it is this inherited approach to food that will form the backbone of this book. Every recipe you will encounter here has either been passed down to me from generations and generations of brilliant cooks in my family, or has been created by me, for my own immediate family and friends.

You see, it's incredibly important to me that every single dish in this book has already been enjoyed heartily at my own kitchen table. For me there are two defining ingredients to every meal in my house: either there has to be a story *behind* it, or, better still, after wiping away tears of laughter, a story (or stories) must *come out* of it.

Just as this brave new world has been opened to me, so too I hope that by opening the pages of my book you will feel as though *you* have been invited to one of the noisiest, funniest and tastiest family meals around.

The Original Chicken Run

Before embarking on this culinary voyage, let me tell you a quick story about how the Sawalhas came to find themselves living and growing up in the leafy (and not so leafy) streets and neighbourhoods between Croydon and Streatham. Food, as you will quickly discover, has been instrumental in our destinies from the very beginning.

My grandmother, Julia Sawalha, was a formidable woman who found her own unique ways to operate in a man's world. And believe me, there was no world more male than that of 1930s Jordan. My father's mother was a brave, domineering and fiercely ambitious woman who could turn her hand to whatever business she wished and invariably made a success of it.

When I was growing up, my father talked of her as though she was a superhero — a woman capable of punching above her weight, muscling her way into the masculine worlds of business, property and politics. Orphaned as a small child, she quickly learned how to duck, dive and manipulate in order to survive. She was a tough woman, but what she lacked in emotional warmth she made up for in sheer single-mindedness.

Her first port of call was always her family, and boy did she have high ambitions for them! In fact, you could say that she was one of the original pushy stage mothers. She shrewdly dedicated her working life to ensuring that her children would never go without in the way she'd had to as a little girl.

Of all her children, I suspect my father may have been her favourite. He was also the one who first showed some acting promise. And so, when the breadth of his talent clearly meant he had to travel beyond the walls of Amman, my grandmother (plucky as ever) secured his ticket out by (wait for it) … roasting 'many, many chickens'!

You see, she knew that she needed to make more money and she needed to make it fast. Back then, like today, land meant money, so she came up with a simple (and highly illegal) plan to convince the authorities that she owned more land than she actually did. To do so she had to find and secure countless witnesses to testify in court that, yes, she had indeed worked and tilled this or that particular strip of previously unclaimed land. If she could 'prove' she worked it, then the court would legally sanction her ownership of it and suddenly she would have a vast portfolio of untouched but highly valuable real estate.

So for a few weeks, in her bid to win over some of the most influential eye-witnesses in the region, a steady flow of tribal heads, council officials and lawyers passed through my grandmother's kitchen, where she presided over a never-ending supply of her perfectly roasted chicken.

Now, you have to understand, my grandmother's roast chicken was so utterly delicious that it made anyone who ate it literally weak at the knees. One bite of her perfect poultry and the unwitting victim left himself utterly vulnerable to her powers of persuasion. And, sure enough, in a matter of weeks various officials had all gone to court swearing blind that they had seen my grandmother 'with their very own eyes', working the land 'night *and* day'!

Week after week, acre after acre of land was gradually rubber-stamped 'Mrs Julia Sawalha', eventually giving her enough money to secure my father a one-way plane ticket to — well, OK, not exactly Hollywood, but drama school in ... Sidcup! Oh yes, and she gave him £30 cash to start him off in his new life — and that was it!

To this day, whenever I get a roast chicken out of the oven, my father always smiles and says, cheekily, 'You know, Nadia, it was a roast chicken that flew me all the way to Sidcup ...'

So that's how we got here in the first place. But who are we? Let me introduce The Family — a long and eccentric cast list whose unique voices and opinions you will find chiming throughout the pages of this book.

Teta (Arabic for 'granny') in the seventies, cooking in the kitchen of her hotel!

My Family

Grandmother Julia
*'My dear, he cannot marry this woman
—she is very mean with her meat.'*
*'Nadia … haraam [poor thing]. At your
age, I was twice your beauty!'*

Auntie Jamileh
*'All day I have been crying, my dear.
We didn't eat well. That woman
brought us one lamb only to the
table! We were left hungrrry!'*

Dad
*The larder is the greatest pharmacy.
And Nadia, believe me, stuffed vine
leaves saved your life!'*

Uncle Nabil
*'I am having a small party,
for just a hundred, maybe
a hundred and fifty.'*

Mum
*'If I have to eat one more flaming
plate of melokhia I'll bloody well
throttle someone!*

Cousin Nayef
*'My Gaard! So lovely to seee you!
You look awful! What have
you been eating?'*

Me

Older Sister Dina
*'I'd spend my last fiver in the world
on a ball of mozzarella.'*

Nephew Zak (age 18)
*'Does anyone fancy a Nando's?
Or a kebab … KFC … jerk
chicken …?'*

Nephew Finlay (age 9)
*'Anyone want to try some Atomic
Waste? It's like extra-hot mint
flavour, but times three! It's
brilliant! As soon as you put
it in your mouth you have
to spit it out!'*

Daughter Maddie (age 6)
*'I love rice and basghetti. But I
want to marry basghetti!'*

Nanny Thelma (a truly great Great-Grandmother)
'Naddy, you're creating a rod for your own back! Tell the lot of 'em to just eat what they're flaming well given and have done with it!'

Nanny Di (a mother-in-law, but also a … human dustbin)
'No, don't throw it away … that can be Thursday's breakfast … Friday's supper … or Sunday's brunch.'

Mark (my irate husband)
'I'm telling you, it might say 'organic' on the packet, but it's a total con, just like getting fifteen per cent extra for free. It's not free. It's just fifteen per cent closer to what it should bloody well cost in the first place!'

Younger Sister Julia
'You see, my system can only really tolerate organic, totally raw food … You couldn't get us a small bag of Monster Munch when you're out could you … ?'

Stepdaughter Issy (age 16)
'Honestly! I just don't see the point of broccoli! It's sooo disgusting!'

Stepdaughter Fleur (age 11)
'I'm not hungry … [5 minutes later] … Is there anything to eat? I'm staaaarrving.'

Daughter Kiki (age 2)
'Mommie, I'se hungee. I want bread honey.'

The Key Ingredients to My Family

I am forty-three years old and now know for sure that I come from a family of nutcases, but, in spite of this, I had a happy childhood. My mother and father were an odd coupling. He (Nadim) grew up in a Bedouin tent in the Jordanian desert and she (Roberta, or Betty for short) started life in a three-bedroom semi in leafy Surrey. By all accounts, their eyes met over an Irish stew in the BBC canteen and, as my mother rather emphatically states, it was love at first sight — on *her* side. Apparently it took a further six years before *he* saw the light. At the time my father was working as a producer and broadcaster for the BBC Arabic Service, part of the organization's Overseas Service, and my mother was a secretary for the French Service, though she got herself transferred to my dad's department the day after she first clapped eyes on him. Dad eventually capitulated (over how many Irish stews I can't begin to imagine), and my two sisters and I arrived a few years later, to be brought up in a variety of *delightful* areas in South London: Brixton, Tulse Hill and sunny Streatham (aka Upper Norwood).

Dad acting his moustache off for the BBC Arabic Service in the sixties.

Mum in Jordan, 1966.

Mum

Whenever I look back on my childhood, it's never long before my mind settles on culinary matters – hardly surprising, given that my mother, with her French ancestry, has always adored all things food-related. Like a flashback in a movie, when I think back to Mum's kitchen, her vast collection of cookery books immediately floats past the end of my nose, flicking and flapping their pages, teasing me with their tasty promises. Mum was always 'on the go' around food, always busy, always mobile. Whether she was jumping on the bus to go to the markets of Croydon to source the freshest British fruit and veg, or heading off on her weekly sojourn to France to purchase slightly more exotic cheeses, meats and pastries, Mum wasn't your average mumsy cook. There was nothing 'ordinary' or 'mundane' about her food.

With my father's Arabic foodie heritage always at the fore, Mum became an experimenter in the kitchen. We never had the same meal twice in a six-month period. When we arrived home from school there was no guessing what she would have magicked up for our beady eyes and growling tummies.

If she wasn't cooking, she was talking about cooking. If she wasn't reading a novel, she had her nose buried in her Elizabeth David. And if she wasn't working away in her kitchen, she was invariably out and about with her best friend Julie, trying out new restaurants and bistros, at a time when the whole notion of eating out was a truly exciting prospect.

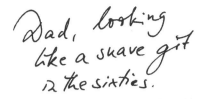

Dad, looking like a suave git in the sixties.

One of Dad's audition photos, taken in... Regent's Park!

Dad

For my father, food has always been a spiritual thing. It is about much, much more than simply filling your stomach. In fact, when I was a young girl and my sisters and I did that wonderfully indulgent thing known as 'scoffing', he would despair and wonder how on earth he was responsible for bringing 'three Hoovers' into the world.

Memories of Dad and food are strangely very Zen-like. He was always a very quiet, very neat, very still diner. More often than not he would occupy a corner of a table or sit in the corner of a room, like a strange woodland animal seeking sustenance from a wide range of little piles of this and that. He's still like this. Only the other day my elder daughter Maddie remarked, 'Teddy [that's the kids' nickname for him] really likes nuts and seeds, doesn't he?' And she's so right. Wherever Dad has been he leaves behind him little dusty pyramids of leftover husks, seed pods, grains and spices.

Alongside his day job, Dad was also an actor and appeared in countless TV dramas. Gradually he became a successful (constantly in work) full-time actor, doing his fair share of big-budget glossy movies. So successful was he at pitching his family 'tent' in the UK, that slowly, in true Bedouin style, over the years a steady flow of relations migrated here, thus transforming a small corner of South-east London into downtown Amman.

Auntie Jamileh

By far the craziest member of the tribe was Auntie Jamileh, who through sheer self-belief and dogged determination might as well have erected her own Bedouin 'tent', by buying the semi next door to us. I remember how I would often lie up in my bedroom, under the open window, inhaling the exotic smells that wafted in from her kitchen down below, dreaming up my own mouthwatering recipes, all the while entertained by the sounds of her muttering, punctuated by hisses, whooshes and those wonderful crackles and fizzles that are the mainstay of cooking fabulously tasty food.

After Mum, my Auntie Jamileh was the biggest culinary influence on our household. She ruled her kitchen with an iron rolling-pin, and woe betide anyone who didn't think her food was manna from heaven. If you had no response to her melokhia, she would consider you nothing more than 'a donkey'. (Believe me, this is a *serious* Arabic insult.)

But, remember! You can never *pretend* to Jamileh that you like things. No. In fact, it's common knowledge throughout the family that she is truly psychic. My husband Mark, who has met her only twice, was truly petrified when first introduced. 'Her eyes bore into your soul,' he said on our wedding day. I corrected him slightly: 'No, sweetheart, her eyes bore into your stomach.' Jamileh knows what your stomach thinks of her food before *you* do. So eating her food is always a mixed bag of pleasure and fear. For Auntie Jamileh, food was, and is, quite literally an extension of herself, the very heart of her. To cut into one of her stuffed aubergines is, in a way, to enter her emotional life … at your peril.

Auntie Jamileh (right) with her sisters-in-law – three great cooks

Dina, Zak and Finlay

Dina is my elder sister. For much of our lives we have lived either together or next door to each other. As a result, her boys feel like my own. As children, it was Dina and I who would cook tasty delights for the rest of the family from the make-believe world of our imaginary television food-show studios. For Christmas and birthdays, we would always buy each other the latest cookbooks; to this day most of my books have Dina's handwritten messages on the front pages, competing with this or that smudge of food. The problem is that I also have an awful lot of cookbooks with my own messages to her in them. You see, as well as buying each other books, we also constantly steal each other's books. I know for certain she has my *Kitchen Diaries*, and until I get it back I'm keeping her *Naked Chef*!

In many ways she was our very own Domestic Goddess: beautiful, glamorous, funny and bloody impressive in the kitchen. Over the years I have always looked up to her, and no acknowledgement of my own cooking credentials can ignore the fact that she was vitally helpful when it came to my winning *MasterChef*.

Dina (left) and me, enjoying some fine dining in southern France.

Our very own superhero, Finlay, in Cornwall.

Zak partaking in a light snack.

Zak is Dina's eldest son and for some strange reason she set him off in the world as a vegetarian, but over the years it would seem the Leo of his birth sign won through, as these days he eats little other than meat (red meat), and lots of it, with the tenacity and concentration of a lion. I adore everything about him. He's devastatingly handsome, well over six feet tall, and a musical genius to boot. He gets extra auntie brownie points because he often says, 'Nanna, you're such a wicked cook!' Believe me, this is high praise indeed from an eighteen-year-old.

Finlay, Dina's youngest, on the other hand, was a proper gourmet baby and used to eat virtually anything *other than* junk food. In fact, he would turn his nose up at anything artificial, so it wouldn't surprise me if he ended up a Michelin inspector. He is an incredibly unique little character, very bright, full of nervous energy, and takes after his granddad in the 'food as a pharmacy' department. If Finlay ever feels poorly or under the weather, he immediately demands a therapeutic chicken soup with fresh vegetables. He says I make the best sarnies in the entire world and is *always* hungry.

Julia

Julia *is* a psychic fairy. Part of me just wants to say that because it's an accurate description. But in her time she has also been known as something of a *psychotic* fairy. At its simplest, Julia is an exciting person to be around. She's fun, she's mad, she's up, she's down — she's *alive*! I love her to bits. When we were children Julia's favourites were sfeeha, mussakhan and (my other childhood favourite) crisp sandwiches. Bizarrely — and ironically — *foie gras* pâté and frogs' legs were on her menu a *lot* when she was growing up. I say bizarrely and ironically because she has, over the years, predominantly been a vegetarian. So it seems other-worldly to remember a childhood in which Julia used to indulge in huge fry-ups and piles of bacon sarnies.

Perhaps her most major meat relapse occurred when working on the film *Chicken Run,* in which she played the voice of a ... chicken! She found herself dreaming, three nights in a row, that she went down to the kitchen and savaged chickens in the fridge. After the third night she was convinced it was a message that she needed protein. The rest was history. She was fully bingeing on poultry and bacon every day and night, until a few months later, holidaying in Spain, she thought, 'Well, I'm eating chicken, so I may as well eat steak.' When it arrived, the meat was still attached to almost the entire ribcage of the dead animal. Within minutes she did a rapid bungee jump back to veggie-ness!

However, over the past two years she really has turned a corner. With the discipline of an entire army of SAS marines, she's committed herself to a raw vegan diet. I'm happy that she's happy, but — I have to say — I really miss cooking for her.

Mark

I met my husband, Mark, eight years ago and food has been a strange affair for us. Our first date was in a beautiful Lebanese restaurant in Battersea. I was so nervous, and after the event I learned that he was too. Not surprising, really, because when I turned up to meet him (having very quickly downed two large vodkas before leaving home), there he was, sitting alone at the table with the largest and most dramatic gash in the world running across his forehead! As he tried to explain that he'd caught it on a deceptively low ceiling at some party in Bristol the night before, I began to laugh. Now, I'm always being told off for laughing at the most inappropriate of moments — but, in my defence, this felt like a totally *appropriate* moment to roar uncontrollably. The only problem was that I didn't stop laughing (appropriately) until we left the restaurant almost 3 hours later. A little disappointed with his first date, Mark declined to 'come back to mine', even though he had a huge and rather presumptuous overnight bag hidden under the table.

In those early years, I used to joke that Mark was *not* a foodie. It is one of the biggest ironies of our marriage that, in the time I've known him, not only has his appreciation of food gradually grown but he has also made some of the most gorgeous food shows I've ever seen. So imagine the pressure when cooking for him now. Not only has it got to taste great, but it has to *look* great too!

That said, I love cooking for him, and whatever he says about my food, I always know what he really thinks. I put an awful lot of love into the food I cook for him, and he assures me he puts an awful lot of love into eating it!

Mark in a restaurant in Buenos Aires. Whilst he reads, I chomp!

Maddie and Kiki

My beautiful, beautiful girls. Let's start with the elder. Maddie: big on personality, low on appetite. It is a great sadness that my dearest Maddie is such a fussy eater. I mean truly fussy. When she first came into the world I held out high hopes for her. She loved olives, hummus and halloumi cheese – even smoked flaming mackerel! And then, *bang*! At the grand old age of three, or possibly four, she hung up her more adventurous side and decided that there were only three things in the world worth living for: mashed potato, white rice and spaghetti (or basghetti) with nothing other than olive oil. She has become a carb hunter! If there's white bread lurking anywhere, she'll smell it out and eat it.

I have to admit, her refusal to eat anything other than white carbs makes me feel like a total failure as a mum. But, for all her resistance at the dining table, she loves helping me in the kitchen and has her own specialities that she likes to cook for her dad. In fact, she makes one of the best rock cakes I have ever tasted in my life. The other night she made half a dozen to take into school. When it came to packing them up, we both followed the trail of crumbs all the way out to her father's car, where he sat grinning like the Cheshire Cat.

Maddie with her daddy's starter.

Kiki gathering herbs for my herby garlic bread.

Kiki, my two-year-old, has a middle name (unlike her older sister). It is simply … Bee. Yes, like a buzzy bee. And never have two names been so appropriate for such a bundle of mischief. She is loud, dramatic, funny, cheeky and mischievous – a Croydon girl sprinkled with fairy dust. More often than not, she's to be seen in her fairy wings, whether it's accompanying her dad to the shops, doing the gardening, going to nursery, or when she climbs into bed. She absolutely *adores* a crowd – or perhaps, God forbid, an audience.

They are my two gifts. However much I daydreamed about being a mum, nothing prepared me for how gorgeous and fabulous my two daughters would be. So imagine how wonderful it is to know that, really, I have *four* daughters. Twice the joy! Half the pushing!

My funky stepdaughters, Issy and Fleur, in sunny Cornwall.

Issy and Fleur

And here are the two that were prepared earlier: Isobel (Issy) and Fleur, so important to me I consider them my own. So let's hurl that 'step' word out the window. These beauties came into my life eight years ago, and I could never imagine life without them. Whenever they trot into my kitchen they're always full of stories, and what I particularly love is that when they are quite literally breathless with having told me what has been going on in their lives, they always ask apprehensively for their favourite dishes — worried I might not have all the right ingredients. Which, let's face it, is never a problem, because their soppy dad will always head straight off to the shops to source whatever is their culinary desire. They both really chuckle about me winning *MasterChef*, because their bedroom is where my trophy resides, on the floor, as a doorstop, invariably with a pair of someone's socks draped over it.

I simply adore cooking them whatever they want, and I'm not like most *step*-mums: I *never* make them eat their greens! Issy and Fleur really come into their own at breakfast. Issy is such a New Yorker — she simply adores her cinnamon and raisin bagels in the morning — whilst Fleur goes into a coma-like silence as (like a Buddhist) she silently and patiently eats her way through piles and piles of pancakes.

Issy's absolute favourites are my jammy duck breasts (funny sounding, I know — but it's what we all call them), my roast potatoes, and (bizarrely) Jaffa Cakes. They also both love packets and packets of Quavers!

Two 'must-haves' for Fleur are spaghetti bolognese and chocolate biscuits. She's always had a good appetite, but in recent years, as we've travelled to places like Morocco, southern Spain and Greece, her culinary curiosity has become really quite impressive. She will try anything once, and more often than not she will come back for more. The only thing I *have* noticed about Fleur's attitude to my cooking is her slightly raised eyebrow at the scale of the mess I leave behind after preparing something as simple as a Quavers sandwich.

Me, Dad and Dina, having just said goodbye to the last of our chickenpox.

When You're Feeling
Under the Weather

Doctor Dad

'We had no antibiotics in the village, but we did have garlic.'
'Parsley is the only Vitamin C your body needs.'

Throughout my childhood, my sisters and I would regularly 'endure' my father expounding the virtues of certain foods' hidden healing powers. Like a magical medieval pharmacist, he would charm us with tales of the mysterious medicinal qualities of everyday ingredients.

In fact, we'd only have to sneeze and the next thing we knew he'd be heading straight to the kitchen, rolling up his sleeves, tying on an apron, barking orders this way and that, as if he were some highly paid surgeon actually heading straight into theatre to perform a life-saving operation. 'Berta [his nickname for my mum]!' he'd shout. 'They have a flooo! We need parsley, plenty of garlic and three eggs.' As he turned the kitchen upside down hunting for these cures, my sisters and I would all chorus in a thick Arabic accent, 'Berta, they must eat *proteeeeein*!' All the while giggling like complete idiots.

My sweet father, oblivious to our mickey-taking, would carry on chopping, whisking, peeling and frying until he had silenced us all with the heavenly aroma of buttery fried eggs, perfectly married with the 'healing' pungency of the 'antibiotic' garlic, finished off with the fresh, full-of-life greenness of the 'vitamin-packed' parsley. As carnage lay around him, he would stand there with a surgeon's concentration, stirring his concoction while the delightful aroma wafted up from his favourite, most trusted and battered old pan.

Invariably, as we sat at the table having scoffed the lot, licking our plates clean, one of us would be cunning enough to cough a little … tiny … cough … 'Berta!' he would shout, leaping to his feet. 'It has spread to their chests! Do we have honey?' At which point, like conspirators, we would all whisper, 'Honey pancakes … Yum.'

The funny thing about Dad was that once he'd 'cured' us with his food, his hypochondria would rear its ugly head and he would end up lying prostrate on the sofa, calling for my mother again. 'Berta, do we have any Beechams?'

Lasagne of Arabia
('For General Weakness of the Body')

The addition of exotic spices to this great Italian classic marries really well with the simplicity of the pasta and the subtle creaminess of the béchamel sauce. If you're unsure whether you *want* to muck about with such a classic, I always say 'A change really can be as good as a rest.'

SERVES 6 (LARGE HELPINGS!)
For the meat sauce
olive oil
1 onion, peeled and very finely chopped
1 heaped tsp each ground cinnamon and ground allspice
450g (1lb) minced beef
3 tbsp tomato purée
salt and black pepper
6 tbsp chopped fresh parsley
15–20 sheets lasagne (the ones that don't require pre-cooking)
For the white sauce
1.2 litres (2 pints) full-fat milk
2 bay leaves
115g (4oz) butter
6 tbsp plain flour
For the topping
85g (3oz) Parmesan, freshly grated

To start the meat sauce, in a heavy-based pan heat a glug or two of olive oil and fry the onion until it's soft. Add the spices and fry until you are hit with the aroma they release, then add the beef and fry until it's browned all over. Now stir in the tomato purée and season to taste with salt and pepper. Add a couple of tbsp water. Leave to simmer away gently for 15–20 minutes.

To make the white sauce, heat the milk with the bay leaves until hot but not boiling, then put to one side. In a heavy-based, non-stick pan, melt the butter over a medium heat. Dust the flour in, whisking constantly until it's smooth. Keep stirring, being careful not to let it brown. Remove the bay leaves from the milk and begin to add the warmed milk slowly, again stirring continuously, until all the milk has been added, then carry on cooking and stirring until the sauce thickens. Season with salt and pepper, and it's ready to go.

Playtime! In an ovenproof dish approximately 38 x 30cm (15 x 12in) spread a couple of tbsp of the meat sauce (it should be quite sparsely spread).

Next, sprinkle on some parsley and then some béchamel sauce, but don't pour it – this is a mistake I've made in the past and I've always ended up with not enough sauce for the top. So, dot 5–6 tbsp of the sauce over the meat, then spread out the sauce with the back of the spoon. Now lay on the dry pasta sheets – my dish needs three to make each layer.

Continue layering the ingredients like this until you have nothing left to play with. Make sure your top layer is béchamel sauce: many a time I have suddenly had to make another batch because I forgot to leave enough for the top.

Sprinkle the grated Parmesan and dot more butter on top, then pop it into the oven at 180°C/gas mark 4 for 40 minutes. To test whether the lasagne is ready, put a sharp knife into the middle: the pasta should be soft.

I find that this tastes even better if it's left to cool down a bit. A mixed salad and my herby garlic bread (see page 62) are a 'must-eat' with this meal.

Garlic and Parsley Omelette

The amounts here are for one omelette. If you're eating this and planning to mix with the outside world, chew some raw parsley afterwards. It'll keep your breath fresh!

SERVES 1–2
4 eggs, beaten with 1 tsp cold water (I know this seems odd,
    but it is what Dad always does)
salt and black pepper
1–2 garlic cloves, peeled and finely chopped (for Dad's
    antibiotic he puts in 3!)
a handful fresh parsley, finely chopped
sunflower or olive oil

Season the eggs with salt and pepper and beat. Gently fry the garlic and parsley in a spot of oil in an omelette pan for a few seconds, then pour in the egg. Fry and flip the omelette as usual.

I love to eat this with simple salted, sliced tomatoes and very buttery bread.

Stuffed Vine Leaves Saved My Life

My father is a hypochondriac, but not of the pill-popping variety. No, he believes that our best medicine cabinet is the larder. In fact, he swears blind that he cured his pre-menstrual tension with turmeric, and yes, I did say pre-menstrual tension. My father has always hated to miss out on any health 'crisis'!

From childhood to the present day I have usually been able to tell from the instant I walk into my parents' kitchen what my dad's illness of the moment is. If raw garlic sandwiches are piled high, he has probably convinced himself he has the flu. If zait wa zaatar (an Arabic breakfast of fresh thyme, toasted sesame seeds and olive oil eaten with pitta and yogurt) is at his elbow, then he is probably petrified he has a chest infection — though more often than not only curried chicken will do for this affliction …

Then there's goat's yogurt and honey for a bad throat and, rather randomly, lasagne for 'general weakness of the body' (I have been known to use this excuse to consume vast quantities of this dish myself). The list is endless — as long as any medical dictionary, to be exact. In fact, now I think of it, he should write his own cookery book!

But my first experience of food as a life-saver revolves around stuffed vine leaves. Or, to quote my father, 'How stuffed vine leaves saved your life'.

Now, these are *not* the ghastly, insipid-tasting vine leaves that you get in the supermarket, with their leathery skins and mashed rice, nor the deliciously tomatoey spicy ones that my aunties back in Jordan would so proudly parade at every wedding, birth and funeral. No, these are the 'anarchic' vine leaves that my mum and dad invented — as Mum says, very simply, 'Just because that's the way we like them', which, when you consider how strictly my Jordanian relations stick to their ancient recipes, was a brave move by Mum and Dad. But that's the thing about my mum. She may be small, but she has culinary balls of steel! She had (and still has) a zero-tolerance policy towards any kind of chilli and so believed that the almost buttery softness of fresh vine leaves needed nothing more than to be stuffed with deliciously melting breast of lamb and fragrant basmati rice, rolled neatly and layered alternately with the lamb bones into that wonderfully old-fashioned piece of kitchen equipment, the pressure cooker. This produced the moistest, most delicately flavoured pile of little green devils imaginable.

Which was just as well, because when I was three years old, suffering from a terrible bout of whooping cough and unable to hold down any food, my dad decided that there was nothing for it but to put me on an intensive course of vine leaves …

So I ate little else for almost two months and, in fact, started to feel much better within days. For years my dad would tell anyone who would listen that it was his stuffed vine leaves that saved my life. What he hadn't reckoned with was that I would never be able to touch the bloody things ever again!

The Stuffed Vine Leaves ...
That Saved My Life!

Every family has its own version of vine leaves: some add spices and herbs; some add more rice than meat; some roll the leaves so tightly you might need a saw to cut through them. The version below is known only to the Sawalha family, London branch, and can be tolerated only by those strong enough to withstand their very unfashionable fat content. All Arabs should look away now: you will *not* like what you see!

If you don't have a vine in your garden — yes, they do grow in England (my mum has one) — use vine leaves from a packet or a jar. Two packets or one jar will yield more than eighty, but a lot will have to be discarded because they're simply too big and tough.

SERVES 4 AS A MAIN DISH

80 medium (about 10cm/4in across) fresh vine leaves, or vine
  leaves preserved in brine
1 large breast lamb, or 2 smaller ones (try to buy breast with the
  flap of meat at the end of the ribs still attached – this will be
  used to make mince for the stuffing. If it has already been cut
  away, use about 350g/12oz shoulder of lamb. Ask the butcher
  to chop through the ribs.)
150g (5½oz) rice (equal parts long-grain and risotto rice)
salt, if necessary
few squeezes lemon juice, if using fresh vine leaves
natural yogurt to serve (optional)

If you're using fresh leaves, blanch in boiling water for a few seconds until they turn from bright green to a brownish green.

If using preserved leaves, separate them and put them in a bowl, cover with boiling water and leave for 10 minutes. Rinse them a few times with cold water to remove some of the brine, then drain. Keep tasting — you don't want them to get too bland.

Cut off the flap from the breast of lamb. If you have a blender, it's your lucky day, because you only have to cut the meat into very small bite-sized pieces and then blend until minced. Without a blender, poor soul, you might need a couple of aunties lurking in the kitchen to help you cut the meat into very small pieces — I'll allow you petits pois-size pieces. It's much

easier to cut the meat if it is very well chilled or even just off frozen. You'll need a roughly equal quantity of meat and rice, so if there isn't enough, you can pare some more meat and fat from the ribs. Don't be squeamish about using the fat: it's important for keeping the rice and leaves juicy.

Wash the rice in hot water first, then rinse it again and again in cold water until the water runs clear. Mix the minced meat and rice together. If you're using preserved leaves you *won't* need salt, as there's enough in the leaves themselves. If you're using fresh ones, salt the rice/meat mixture to taste and add a big pinch to the cooking water.

Lay a vine leaf in front of you, with the raised veiny side up and the stalk end towards you. (If it has a stalk, cut it off.) Take some rice and meat in one hand and squeeze and roll it (not too tightly) into a 1cm (½in) thick, pencil-shaped roll to fit on to the vine leaf with about 1cm (½in) each side to spare when you place it horizontally three-quarters of the way down from the top of the leaf.

Take the piece of leaf nearest to you and fold it over the meat mixture, then fold over the two sides, and roll away from you, as firmly as you can, tucking in the edges as you go to make a neat roll. It's not necessary for the leaves to be exactly the same size, but if you start with one about 10cm (4in) across and use the same amount of stuffing for each one, then the overall result will be that they will all look the same size – *in sha'allah* (hopefully)!

Although we like this to be a fatty dish, there is usually too much fat on the rib pieces, so cut off the large chunks that run along the top end of the bones. Lay two or three bones in the bottom of a pressure cooker or medium-sized heavy saucepan, then layer the rolled leaves, tightly packed together, with two or three bones between each layer, finishing with a layer of bones. If you're using fresh vine leaves, squeeze a little lemon juice over each layer of leaves.

If using a pressure cooker, add 425ml (¾ pint) cold water and bring up to pressure. Simmer for 25 minutes, then turn off the heat and leave, unopened, for half an hour. Drain and turn out on to a large plate to serve. If using an ordinary saucepan, add 600ml (1 pint) cold water, put a weighted plate on top of the vine leaves, bring to the boil and simmer for 50–60 minutes, or until the rice is cooked and the meat tender. Leave covered for 15 minutes before draining and serving.

Natural yogurt is a very good accompaniment.

Teddy Toast

Why 'Teddy' toast? Well, Dad's name is Nadim and Mum's nickname for him is 'Neddy'. When my nephew Zak was a toddler (stick with me on this) he couldn't say 'Neddy', so Dad became 'Teddy' — phew, got there in the end! In fact, my husband has spent years trying to work out everyone's real names. For example, my mum is known to different people as Roberta, Bobby, Berta and Betty. I'm sure when we got married Mark thought he was about to acquire at least three different mothers-in-law!

Anyway, Doctor Dad came up with this recipe for Zak, when he was two years old and refusing to eat anything but pizza. So, basically, this is a super-quick healthy pizza, for which you don't really need specific quantities …

PER PERSON
2 slices wholemeal bread
olive oil
sliced tomato
a sprinkle of zaatar (a unique mix of Arabic herbs, sumac and
   toasted sesame seeds available from Middle Eastern shops),
   or dried thyme or oregano
crushed garlic (optional)
grated Cheddar, or thin slices halloumi cheese

Dad toasts the bread on one side, then brushes the untoasted sides with olive oil. Next he lays the sliced tomatoes on top and sprinkles them with the zaatar and garlic. He always drizzles a little more olive oil over, then tops it all with grated cheese or thin slices of halloumi. Then he grills the lot until the cheese is all melty.

BUT … Approach with caution. In my greed I've often blistered my top lip!

Dad's Chicken Soup Soother

Although I've given you this list of ingredients, if I'm honest I usually use whatever I have hanging about in the fridge. Dad loves to add 'something green' right at the end, 'just so the vitamins aren't boiled away'. Maybe add some spinach or grated courgettes, so long as it's a *greeeen* vegetable; he's *very* specific about that!

SERVES 4–6
2 tbsp olive oil
3 onions, peeled and chopped (medicinal purposes)
4 celery sticks, chopped
4 carrots, peeled and thickly sliced
6 garlic cloves, peeled but left whole (antibiotic Dad's way)
1 fresh chilli, chopped (optional)
1 dsp each ground cumin and ground coriander
1 cardamom pod
2 cinnamon sticks
1 medium-sized chicken, cut into as many pieces as you like
1.7 litres (3 pints) water
salt and black pepper
a large handful vermicelli
a handful baby spinach leaves
chopped fresh parsley
juice of 1 lemon

Pour the olive oil into a large saucepan and fry the onion, celery, carrot, garlic and chilli (if using), until softened. Throw in the spices, give them a stir, then add the chicken. Pour in the water and season well. Bring it all to the boil, then 'turn down the fire' and let it all bubble away for an hour or so.

Take the chicken out and, when cool enough to handle, remove the skin and bones. Shred the meat and pop it back into the soup. Crush the vermicelli in your hand and throw that in too. Bring it back up to the boil, then reduce the heat and simmer until the vermicelli is cooked.

Just before you tuck in, throw in the spinach, sprinkle on the parsley and add a squeeze of lemon juice 'for the extra Vitamin C'.

Zait wa Zaatar (Oil with Herbs)

As a small girl (and now as an adult), watching my father prepare his breakfast was a little like being hypnotized by a snake-charmer. I always marvel at how he appears to be moving in total slow motion — a magically staged bit of acting when I was young, though today I realize it's probably more a case of him trying to remember what comes next.

As with most things edible in my father's life, the preparation of zait wa zaatar is all about keeping healthy. He invariably prepares this deceptively simple little dish either in service of some current ache or pain, or, better still, as a pre-emptive strike against any incoming pains that 'may be in the near vicinity'.

I beg of you: try this for breakfast one day. It is quite, quite delicious and will almost instantly soothe away the day's worries.

SERVES 6–10
Zaatar
6 tbsp each finely ground dried thyme and dried marjoram
1 tbsp sumac (a glorious spice; from Middle Eastern shops)
2 tbsp sesame seeds, toasted

Simply mix all these ingredients together and keep in an airtight container.

Accompaniments
labneh (strained yogurt; from Middle Eastern shops), or Greek yogurt
runny honey
pitta bread (see page 136)
olive oil
olives

So! Let the zait wa zaatar ritual begin … First, Dad always serves himself on an old chipped saucer. It drives Mum nuts. 'Teddy! Do you have to?' Next, he neatly (almost tenderly) places 2 teaspoons of zaatar on the very edge of his saucer (just to the left of the chip in the ceramic). He then lovingly brings 2 spoons of creamy yogurt to rest beside the zaatar (but *not* — I repeat *not* — touching it).

With a graceful arcing movement and from a great height, he pours glistening olive oil over the yogurt. If, however, he has 'a bit of a bad chest', he pours a little golden honey *into* the milky white yogurt.

Next, he tears a piece of warm pitta bread, dipping and swirling it between all the ingredients on the saucer before finally popping it into his mouth and settling down into his chair with a steaming sweet mint tea (see page 268).

The Great Spag 'n' Bol Swindle

OK – well, this isn't exactly a cure for an illness. It's more a way of navigating your way through those hangovers that simply cling on to your skull and won't go away (what we call in our family 'self-inflicted headaches').

Emerge from bed. All bleary-eyed. Think you've got away with things? No sign of pounding brain. Slowly descend the stairs. Bottom step. Foot paused in mid-air. Was that a twinge? No. Nothing. Not yet. It looks like this is going to be one of those boomerang hangovers (comes pinging back at you when you least expect it). So. With limited time in hand, evasive action must be taken. Here's what to do.

Get yourself into the kitchen. Alka-Seltzer. Normally, when I have the time (and the shrill distant tremors of hangover hell aren't on the horizon), I love nothing more than to prepare a slow-cooked ragù sauce using the finest ingredients available to mankind. *This* recipe, however, is for a far cheaper, speedier, easier version, aptly named 'The Great Spag 'n' Bol Swindle'. Simple but delicious, it hails from the days when I was often stony-broke, out nearly every night of the week, with the kind of hangovers that come with spending all your money on horribly cheap alcohol.

I don't know about you, but in my humble opinion spag bol is the ultimate hangover cure, although I have to admit (and please don't judge me on this) that sometimes only a cheese and crisp sandwich will do … Anyway, trust me, the next time you suspect there's a hangover on the way, try taking part in The Great Spag 'n' Bol Swindle. It's *the* perfect weapon for headache interception!

SERVES 4

500g (1lb 2oz) spaghetti

salt and black pepper

For the sauce

400g (14oz) minced beef (if money is tight you could use
    half mushrooms)

olive oil

1 onion, peeled and finely chopped

2 celery sticks, sliced (if you have some, but don't worry
    if it's only a half dead bit – it will still add flavour)

as many garlic cloves as you want (I use 4 or 5), peeled
    and chopped

4 tbsp tomato purée

1–2 sloshes red wine (if not too scarred from the night before)

400g (14oz) can chopped tomatoes

a big pinch dried oregano

(cheffy types look away) 1 Oxo cube (Aaaaahhhh!)

a little water

To serve

chopped parsley

cheese, of course, is always gorgeous with spag bol
    (adjust according to the predicted scale of your hangover)

In your favourite pan (with hangover imminent, my favourite pan is like a comfort blanket), put the mince and dry-fry it until it's browned. Remove and put to one side.

Now pour a couple of glugs of olive oil into the pan. (The sound should remind you of the third or fourth bottle of Chianti from the night before!) Throw in the onion and celery and fry gently until transparent. Stir a few times (black bits don't really work too well here!), then add the garlic and stir again. I always add the tomato purée here and fry it until it darkens in colour and the aroma changes. I find this really deepens the flavour.

Tip in the meat. Now (if you're not yet feeling the tremors) is a good time to add the wine. Bring the heat up a touch to burn off the alcohol (no bad thing). Add the tomatoes, oregano, crumbled Oxo cube, and some salt and pepper. Reduce the heat and let it all pop and bubble away for 30–60 minutes, depending on how severe your headache is. Whilst waiting, take another Alka-Seltzer just to maintain your (by now) uncontrollable hunger. Add some water if it starts to dry out a bit.

Cook the spaghetti in boiling salted water according to packet instructions and drain. Serve each portion of pasta topped with some sauce. Sprinkle with parsley and cheese.

My herby garlic bread (see page 62) goes really well with this.

Easy-peasy Yummy Chicken Curry

This is an essential 'first-sign-of-a-cold' recipe. My dad has always sworn blind that plenty of garlic, ginger and onions can kill a cold stone dead, so I invented this with him in mind, though it's rapidly become my husband's lunch of choice.

I couldn't agree more with Dad about this curry's recuperative powers, except *I* believe that sipping a glass of red wine (or two) can add enormously to the medicinal powers of this particularly spicy dish.

SERVES 3–6

6 chicken breasts or legs (be careful if you use breasts as
   they can dry out easily)
vegetable oil
2 medium onions, peeled and chopped
6 garlic cloves, peeled and finely chopped
5cm (2in) piece fresh root ginger, grated
2 tbsp Madras curry paste (Patak's is a good one)
1 dsp tomato purée
100ml (3½ fl. oz) water
a couple of glugs double cream
2–3 tbsp chopped fresh coriander
1 tbsp nigella seeds (black onion seeds; from Indian shops),
   fried in a little oil (these give a really authentic flavour)

If you don't have time to fry the chicken, just remove the skin and add the chicken pieces to the sauce. Otherwise, heat 2 or so tsp of the oil in a large, lidded frying pan and brown the chicken pieces. Remove and put to one side.

In the same pan, fry the onions until just golden, then add the garlic and ginger and fry until soft-ish.

Time for the curry paste: stir this into the onion mixture until the aroma intensifies. Add the tomato purée and stir until it starts to change colour. Add the chicken, pour in the water and bring to the bubble, then let it all simmer away under a lid until the sauce is reduced and the chicken is meltingly soft. If the sauce looks a bit thin, take off the lid and let it reduce.

Stir in the cream, and garnish with lots of chopped fresh coriander and the fried nigella seeds.

An Arabian
Sunday Lunch

Your Average Sawalhas' Sunday Lunch

It's a beautiful Sunday morning. I'm twelve years old and feeling just great. Why? There's a family outing planned to my Auntie Jamileh's house. She's just returned from a two-month trip to Jordan and is desperate to cook for the London branch of the Sawalhas. The great thing about any trip to my Auntie Jamileh's is that it doesn't take long — she lives next door!

We hammer on the door, she flings it open and proceeds to bite and squeeze our cheeks while showering us with noisy, lip-smacking kisses (this bit was always more than a little annoying). As we wriggle, escape and run through the hall, we trip over her open suitcases.

In the kitchen there'd already be an incredible din, as more often than not my uncles, aunties and cousins would all be arguing about everything, from what plates the food should be served on to the rather more *complicated* subject of Middle Eastern politics.

As my sisters and I entered this hubbub of affectionate adult conflict, our childish play was forever being stalled as they interrupted their grown-up conversations to shower us with kisses, hugs and often-painful tweaks of the cheeks. Then, as if under starters' orders, they'd all turn back to their respective bossing or rowing as if we girls had simply vanished into thin air.

I didn't mind though. This sudden invisibility was often my cue to have a good nose around. First I'd explore the hob, lifting the lids on bubbling pots of lamb and cumin stew; steaming pots of cabbage leaves stuffed with spicy meat, rice, garlic and mint (so delicious!); huge pans of simmering melokhia and chicken (my mum's most hated dish, but everyone else's favourite); and for any (very frowned upon but begrudgingly tolerated) vegetarians, a dish that was prettily known as the 'lentil dream'.

At the centre of all this activity were bowls and trays of variously cored and stuffed vegetables. You name it, Jamileh stuffed it. These flavour-packed veggie grenades of succulence looked like the crown jewels at the centre of a royal party.

Next it would be the wonders of the oven. Here I pull out a tray of kibbeh (a delicious concoction of lamb, burghul wheat, onions and pine nuts mixed together and baked), then I get hold of a tray of my favourite mini meat pizzas (or sfeeha), at which point the kitchen again erupts into a cacophony of Arabic and English shouting. Not angry shouting – simply passionate and unmistakably Arabic!

Cousin Nayef: 'Hurry. My God! People are hungry! Good God, the child [me exploring] is in the oven!'

Auntie Jamileh, now on the defensive: 'It's ready! I am waiting for *you*! You never stop talking and people need to be fed!' Jamileh appears to be offended, and we all giggle at how silly they sound.

Cousin Laurice: 'Don't, Yamma [Arabic for 'mother']. Don't make yourself angry – the food will go cold! We will never eat!'

I stand there wide-eyed, a little unsure which way this could go. With everyone's eyes bulging and voices a little strained, it feels as though this could turn into family fisticuffs. As if to confirm this possibility, Auntie Jamileh suddenly raises herself to her full 4 foot 10, apparently preparing to throw a punch. Like those ludicrously brave soldiers in films who throw themselves on hand grenades in order to save everyone else, I use my body to intercept her, flinging my arms around her and saying, in my sweetest of sweet voices, 'But you've worked so hard, Auntie, and it looks soooo delicious, please can we eat now? Pleeease?'

Everyone holds his or her breath. For a moment we don't know which way this could go – and suddenly she beams at me, 'Haraam [poor thing],' and caresses my face. 'Of course, habibti [darling].'

Then she shouts so loudly it virtually floors me, 'Come on, everyone – time to eat!' And with that, the entire family piles into the dining room, armed with knives, pots, pans and trays, descending on the dining table like an army of singing, bickering, bossy Bedouin warriors – which I guess is exactly what they all are.

The feast that was Your Average Sawalha Sunday Lunch had begun, and if you were a guest, you'd more than likely hear the following sentence whispered conspiratorially into your left ear …

'My Dear, I Have Never Met a Vegetable I Couldn't Stuff'

Let me tell you a secret about my Auntie Jamileh. She has a powerful and all-consuming passion: she cannot see a vegetable without getting an irresistible urge to stuff it! This is no exaggeration. So committed is she to the act of filling delicious veggies with ever more divine flavours that she has in her time not only stuffed the likes of aubergines, peppers and tomatoes but, with her appetite for breaking culinary boundaries, she's also managed to stuff carrots, turnips and parsnips. Amazingly, she was the first woman in Jordan to stuff a cucumber successfully (there's a photo of it on her wall).

Yep, all these vegetables have fallen victim to my Auntie Jamileh's compulsion. But her drive isn't simply an eccentric one. The reason she's driven to do it is because, basically, a pot of stuffed vegetables in Jordan is the most prized of family meals. In fact, Dad always says that it is equivalent in importance to a British roast dinner, adding, rather snootily, 'But of course, it is farrrr more delicious!'

Great kudos is therefore attached to those mothers who make the very finest stuffed vegetables, and as far as my Auntie Jamileh is concerned she absolutely makes the finest. My father's cousin Nael was once so convinced that *his* mother made the finest stuffed vegetables that he went to the extraordinary lengths of paying for his younger brother to bring a pot of them on his lap, by plane, all the way from Jordan to London. By all accounts, Nael, so desperately homesick and keen to taste his mother's cooking, proceeded to eat the lot, straight from the pot, on a bench outside Heathrow's Terminal 3 arrivals (I kid you not).

So, although Auntie Jamileh's stuffing addiction verges on total madness, it is, thankfully, accompanied by some delicious stuffings: lamb, spices, rice, maybe some nuts, all of them cooked slowly until they're meltingly soft (not a politically correct crisp vegetable in sight).

The culinary significance of stuffed veggies cannot be exaggerated. It's a way of life, a show of love and a confirmation of status — which may explain why, the last we heard from Jamileh, she was in her kitchen trying to hollow out and fill a Brussels sprout!

Stuff Ya Potatoes!

Jamileh spent a month finding out how to stuff potatoes in this way. And they're *delicious*, especially with buttered cabbage and onions sitting prettily alongside them.

SERVES 2 BIG EATERS
8 potatoes, peeled (I use Maris Piper)
sunflower oil
butter
olive oil
2 tbsp chopped fresh coriander or parsley
For the filling
4 tbsp pine nuts
1 medium onion, peeled and chopped
1 tsp ground cinnamon
2–3 tsp ground allspice
225g (8oz) organic minced lamb (not lean – a bit of fat
   really adds flavour)
2 tomatoes, finely chopped
salt and black pepper
3 tbsp tomato purée
300ml (½ pint) lamb stock, hot

Preheat the oven to 180°C/gas mark 4.

Cut a piece off the top of each potato, so that you leave an area big enough to core out the centre and leave a 1cm (½in) thick wall. Discard the cored-out part. Now heat a little sunflower oil and a knob of butter and fry the potatoes until golden brown. Put to one side.

For the filling, heat some sunflower oil in a heavy-based frying pan, throw in the pine nuts and fry until coloured. Put to one side.

Fry the onion in the same pan until soft, adding a little more oil if necessary, then add the spices and fry until their aroma is released. Now stir in the lamb, tomatoes and pine nuts. Season well. Turn off the heat.

Fill the prepared potatoes with the gorgeously spicy lamb mixture, leaving a 1cm (½in) gap at the top. Lay them side by side in a suitably sized oven dish. Mix the tomato purée with the hot lamb stock and pour around the potatoes. It should come halfway up the potatoes; add a little hot water if it doesn't. Cover with foil and bake for 45–50 minutes, or until tender. Take the foil off and drizzle some olive oil over for the last 15 minutes.

Serve sprinkled with coriander or parsley.

Stuff Ya Courgettes!

If you can get pale green courgettes, that would be so much nicer than dark green — they're fatter and easier to hollow out, and somehow just taste better. You can find them in Turkish or Middle Eastern shops.

SERVES 2 GOOD EATERS
1kg (2¼lb) medium courgettes
salt and lots of black pepper
For the filling
200g (7oz) minced lamb (not lean – a bit of fat adds flavour)
85g (3oz) short-grain rice, washed and drained
1 tbsp tomato purée
2 tsp baharat spice mix (see page 120)
3 tbsp chopped fresh coriander
1 garlic clove, peeled and crushed
For the sauce
olive oil
6 whole garlic cloves, peeled
2 tbsp tomato purée
400g (14oz) can chopped tomatoes
15g (½oz) butter
300ml (½ pint) water
4 tbsp lemon juice, mixed with 2 crushed garlic cloves (optional)

For the filling, mix the lamb with the rice and all the remaining stuffing ingredients, and season really well with salt and pepper.

With a corer, remove the middle of the courgettes and fill the courgettes with the stuffing, tapping gently on the base to shake the filling down. Leave at least a 2.5cm (1in) gap at the top because, if you overfill them, like the carrots, the courgettes may split as the rice puffs up.

In a wide saucepan with a lid, heat a few glugs of olive oil and fry the whole garlic cloves for a minute or so, stir in the tomato purée and tomatoes, along with the butter and water, then season well. Bring almost to the boil, then lay the courgettes in the sauce. Add a little more water so that they are completely covered. Put a tightly fitting lid on. Bring to the boil, then simmer very slowly for about 45–60 minutes, or until the rice is cooked. I nurse these babies quite a bit, turning them, adjusting the seasoning, etc.

When the time is up, if using, add the lemon juice and crushed garlic and simmer for another 5 minutes.

Stuff Ya Carrots!

As you can imagine, you will need really big carrots for this recipe so that you have half a chance of stuffing them. Don't ask me why, but I have found that Chinese supermarkets sell absolutely ginormous ones. In this recipe I cook the carrots in a tamarind-paste sauce which gives the dish a slightly sweet-and-sour flavour.

SERVES 4

1kg (2¼lb) large carrots
vegetable oil and a little butter for frying the carrots (you don't have to fry them, but my God, they taste good if you do)
2 tbsp tamarind paste, dissolved in about 900ml (1½ pints) water
1 tbsp salt

For the filling
85g (3oz) short- or medium-grain rice
2 tsp salt
2 tbsp vegetable oil
250g (9oz) minced lamb
1 tsp ground cinnamon
2 tsp ground allspice
½ tsp cardamom seeds, crushed

Peel the carrots, rinse them and scoop out the insides (that sounds simple, doesn't it!). If you can't get hold of the special corer they use in the Middle East — a long, slim, sharp instrument of vegetable torture - you can use an apple corer (though it *will* be tricky).

To prepare the filling, wash the rice and allow it to soak for 30 minutes in tepid water with 1 tsp of the salt added. Drain and mix with the other filling ingredients, including the other tsp of salt.

Put the stuffing into the carrots, leaving about a 2.5cm (1in) gap at the top. Don't push down on it too hard or the carrots will split when the rice cooks.

Fry the carrots gently in a little oil (and, if you fancy, a little butter to add flavour) until lightly browned, then arrange in a wide pan. Dissolve the tamarind paste in the water and pour over the carrots. Add the salt (what a lot!). Cover and bring to the boil, then reduce the heat to very low and cook for 40–60 minutes, or until the carrots are tender and the rice is cooked.

Malfouf *(Stuffed Cabbage Leaves Save the Day)*

This dish was always made by the women in the family, amongst a cacophony of chit-chat and gossiping. Not only was it a total crowd-pleaser at the dining table, but it was also a massive crowd-pleaser in the kitchen. My sisters and I would always stay *very* close to the women cooking these buttery soft rolls, quite simply because the chit-chat was some of the most entertaining and colourful we'd ever heard in our young lives!

If ever there was a dish that should have been made by me and all my co-hosts on *Loose Women*, this was it. If there is ever an Arabic version of the programme, the best way to guarantee the most scintillating chat and gossip would be to plonk the ingredients listed below in front of the women and simply get them to cook malfouf. I'm telling you, they'd seriously spill the beans!

SERVES 4

150g (5½oz) round-grain rice

1 large Cypriot cabbage, about 2kg (4½lb) (from Middle Eastern shops, but if you can't find any, ordinary white cabbage can be used instead)

salt and black pepper (remembering the stock will be salty)

juice of 1 lemon (half to go in with the cabbage, half at the end)

1 large garlic clove, peeled and finely chopped

1 tsp ground cinnamon

250g (9oz) minced lamb

butter

225ml (8 fl. oz) stock (made from the cabbage-blanching water and 1 tbsp lamb stock concentrate)

1 tbsp pomegranate syrup (from Middle Eastern/Turkish shops or large supermarkets)

For the pouring sauce

juice of 1 lemon

2–3 garlic cloves, peeled and very finely chopped

2 tbsp tepid water

Wash the rice in hot water first, then rinse it in cold, a couple of times; the water doesn't have to run clear. Leave it to soak for 30 minutes.

Cut the leaves from the stem of the cabbage one by one, peeling them off very carefully so you don't split them. Cut them into squares of about 13cm (5in): no need to be prissy about it — they can be rough and ready.

Bring a large saucepan of water to the boil and add 1 tbsp salt and the juice of half the lemon. Throw in the cabbage leaves a few at a time and blanch for about a minute, until just beginning to soften. Put each batch into a colander to drain. Keep the blanching water for the stock.

Drain the rice and mix with the garlic, cinnamon, some salt and plenty of black pepper, then mix the lamb in thoroughly with your hands.

Lay a square of cabbage in front of you. Squeeze a bit of the rice/lamb mixture into a thickish chipolata shape about 8cm (3in) long and put it just inside the nearest side of the cabbage leaf. Roll away from you until it is completely rolled. Do the same with the remaining leaves until all the filling has been used.

The number you get will simply depend on the size and ambition of the cabbage!

Save a few leaves to line the bottom of a heavy, buttered casserole dish (it must have a tight-fitting lid). Arrange the rolled leaves close together in the dish in layers, squeezing over the remaining lemon juice. Mix the stock with the pomegranate syrup and pour this over the layers.

Put a heatproof plate on top of the leaves, pressing them well down, and then put a weight on top. Bring to the boil and cook, covered, on medium heat for 30 minutes, checking from time to time that the water hasn't dried up. Now turn the heat to a very slow simmer and cook for another 15 minutes. Then take one stuffed cabbage leaf out and try it to make sure the rice is cooked through.

Turn the rolled leaves out of the pot on to a serving plate. They should, if you're very lucky, have absorbed all the water and come out like a cake.

Mix together the lemon juice, garlic and water in a small jug and offer it round for people to drizzle on the cabbage leaves. Mmmmm.

Melokhia

(Egyptian Leaf Soup – You'll Either Love It or Hate It)

This is an absolute staple of Arabic meals. It really is what I call the Marmite dish of Arabic cuisine. Every single Arabic woman in the family has her own very specific way of making it and every time we all gather, there's always a big discussion beforehand about who exactly is responsible for it.

Unbeknownst to the Arab women in the family, this dish has become a real bone of contention between Mum and Dad. In fact, over the years they have had more rows about this 'peasant-style Arab soup' than about anything else. If anything could have ripped their loving and devoted fifty-year marriage to shreds, it's their totally divided opinions on melokhia.

Whenever Mum remarks on how horrid the dish is, she chooses some of the most extraordinarily 'colourful' language available to mothers. Dad, bless him, always adopts an aggressive tribesman's stance and proceeds to mount a defence of this Egyptian classic. It really is a miracle their marriage has survived it. Whilst Dad always ends up going on about how it pre-dates the Pyramids, Mum just sits back with a bee in her bonnet, a glass of gin in her hand, jabbing back, 'Yes! And it tastes as old as the ruddy Pyramids! I am *not* eating it, let alone cooking it!'

Melokhia ('Jew's Mallow') is a kind of Middle Eastern bitter spinach – definitely an acquired taste. It doubles as a fabulous natural thickening agent. It's quite difficult to find it fresh outside the Middle East, but it can be bought dried in some Turkish or Middle Eastern shops.

First you'll need some good chicken stock (ideally, better than a stock cube), so try to make your own – it's really simple. Throw a small chicken into a big pan of water – you need to be left with 1.2–1.7 litres (2–3 pints), so top up as you go – and simmer for a couple of hours with some chopped onion, celery and carrot, a chopped garlic clove, 1 tbsp ground coriander and 1 tsp cayenne pepper, salt and black pepper.

SERVES 6
1kg (2¼lb) chicken, quartered
salt and white pepper
sunflower oil
1 large onion, peeled and roughly chopped
1 whole garlic bulb, peeled and crushed
1 tbsp ground coriander
85g (3oz) dried melokhia leaves, lightly crushed (from Middle
    Eastern/Turkish shops)
1.2–1.7 litres (2–3 pints) chicken stock (see above)
For the side sauce
2 medium onions (preferably red), peeled and roughly chopped
2 tsp sumac (from Middle Eastern shops)
375ml (13 fl.oz) cider vinegar

Fry the chicken pieces with a dash of salt and some white pepper in 2 tbsp oil until nicely browned. Remove from the pan. Fry the onion in the same pan — you might need to add some more oil — until just translucent. Add the crushed garlic and coriander and fry gently until the garlic begins to turn golden.

Meanwhile, put the melokhia leaves into a large saucepan and just cover with some of the stock you have made ... Oh, all right, you couldn't be bothered, so use a good bouillon or stock cube. Bring to the boil, then simmer gently for 15 minutes.

Now add the chicken, together with the fried onion mixture, and top up with stock to cover — but not too much, as the sauce must remain quite thick. Simmer for another 40 minutes.

For the side sauce, put the onions in a blender until just chopped; don't let them turn into a purée. Stir in the sumac, place in a bowl and just cover with cider vinegar. Everyone helps themselves to a spoonful or two to stir into their melokhia.

Serve with rice.

Auntie Jamileh's Sfeeha ... Almost!

'My dear! No one can cook food as delicious as mine! No one!'
'She is a very bad woman. She can't cook, for God's sake!'

When I was a child, I spent a lot of time with Auntie Jamileh. And, before going much further, I think it would be fair to say that she's always been something of a nutcase. Her temperament was (and still is) frighteningly fierce, and it was never fiercer than when she was cooking, especially when she was cooking *her own* recipes.

In fact, it's common knowledge within my family that if you ask Auntie Jamileh for one of her recipes, she will smile at you (almost sweetly), shift around uncomfortably in her chair (sometimes hiding a container of a new-found spice behind a cushion) and then proceed slowly, and I mean slowly, to talk you through it. Now when I say 'talk you through it', I mean she will take you on a 45-minute journey through countless other recipes, anecdotes and total flights of fancy in an attempt to disorientate, confuse, dazzle and mystify you. If you stay on your toes, you will walk away feeling a certain smug certainty that you have managed to cobble together the bare bones of one of her recipes.

But – be warned. 'Cunning' is a word you could easily apply to Auntie Jamileh, because once home, kitchen in total disarray, the remnants of her spoken recipe jotted down on a piece of paper – you discover (often at the critical point of serving up) that she has *always* left a crucial little something out of her instructions. This is my Auntie Jamileh's act of recipe sabotage! She effectively lays little landmines of culinary confusion that always wreck the dish at hand but, most importantly, preserve the preciousness and exclusivity of her kitchen magic.

As kids, my sisters and I would do almost anything to get her to cook these gorgeous mini lamb pizzas, known in Jordan as 'sfeeha'. We would sit in her kitchen listening to incredible stories of her childhood back in the village, quite literally stuffing dozens of these delicious morsels into our mouths and pockets.

Sfeeha *(Mini Middle Eastern Pizzas)*

So, here is Auntie Jamileh's recipe for sfeeha — though, of course, it took me some time to perfect it, as by my estimates she left out at least three ingredients. I have marked them with asterisks in case you are interested in which ones they were.

I quite often triple these amounts, as I plan to put some in the freezer — well, that's always my *plan* anyway …

MAKES 20–30

For the topping

350g (12oz) lamb mince

2 tsp each ground cinnamon and ground allspice

3 tbsp pine nuts, lightly fried

2 handfuls chopped fresh parsley

2 tsp pomegranate syrup* (from Middle Eastern/Turkish
   shops or large supermarkets)

1–2 tsp salt

1 tsp freshly ground black pepper

1 medium onion, peeled and grated

2 tomatoes, very finely chopped

4 tbsp tahini

2 tbsp lemon juice*

For the dough

1 tsp dried yeast, dissolved with a pinch caster sugar

450g (1lb) strong white bread flour

1½ tsp fine salt

125ml (4 fl. oz) olive oil

175ml (6 fl. oz) plain yogurt* (such a vital one to leave out –
   she is so naughty)

125ml (4 fl. oz) warm water

Put all the topping ingredients in a bowl and mix very well until almost a paste. This is definitely a job for the hands and, yes, it *is* mucky. Pop in the fridge.

Hopefully you have a dough hook, otherwise prepare for a lot of kneading when making the dough. Leave the yeast to dissolve for 5 minutes, or until it starts to bubble. In a large mixing bowl put the flour and salt, making a well in the middle. Add the dissolved yeast, oil and yogurt and mix it all in. It's messy and feels all wrong initially, but trust me, it will be OK! If you're using an electric dough hook, turn it on and, little by little, add some warm water (you may need a bit more or a bit less than you've measured). Whether you are kneading by hand or with a machine, just carry on until you get a smooth elastic dough.

Roll the dough into a ball, put it in a bowl in a warm place, cover it and leave for 2 hours or until doubled in size. Punch it down and leave for another 20–30 minutes.

Meanwhile, preheat the oven to 230°C/gas mark 8.

On a floured surface roll out the dough and divide it into about 30 pieces. Roll them out into rough circles. Don't be too fussy about this – the more rustic and uneven the better. Now take a spoonful of the lamb mixture and flatten it on to the dough, taking it right up to the edges, as it shrinks a fair bit.

Put the sfeeha on to a baking tray and pop them into the oven for 20–30 minutes. The dough should still be pale.

Auntie Jamileh would always make a huge salad to go with these gorgeous little pizzas. Sfeeha really were my favourite childhood dish. I urge you to try them yourself, and am certain any nearby kids will love them too.

Jamileh holding court.

Journey to the Centre of Mother's Kitchen

As a child I just loved Sundays, whiling away the hours curled up on my mother's antique rocking chair, leafing through her varied selection of well-worn cookery books and magazines. (Her lemon soufflé (page 261) and pear tart with Armagnac (page 262) are both inspired by recipes from one of these magazines: *Cordon Bleu*.) I can so easily remember the gentle rocking rhythm, the light creak of the floorboards, the feeling of freedom as the pages flicked past — as though I was riding somewhere on a magical time machine. Whenever I went on these journeys I'd hold the book in my hand, close my eyes and, with the back-and-forth motion of the chair, simply wait as the pages flicked to and fro before falling open at one of my mother's well-thumbed favourite recipes. For me, these day-dreamy times were tantamount to riding in my very own horse-drawn carriage to distant, long-forgotten culinary lands.

A regular destination on these journeys was a place called 'Pavlova'. I remember it was on page 72 of a battered old book, with flecks of ancient meringue splattered all over the page, the musky smell of stale vanilla essence rising from the photograph. Another place I'd always pass through was her favourite stew recipe: beautifully patterned with tomatoey oil and dusty flour. What made my journeys so special were these little three-dimensional additions: with every smudge or floury fingerprint, tiny edible tokens of Mum's love and affection for us girls would rise before me and give me a lovely, tingly, warm feeling.

The rocking chair was always in the kitchen, so to find myself in it usually meant it was a Sunday — because this was the day Mum would open the doors to her culinary empire and let us girls in.

I have to say, I will be eternally grateful to her for giving my sister and me carte blanche to create whatever we wanted for that day's lunch. Imagine how exquisite it was, being allowed into this adult world and, what's more, being taken seriously. I hear friends talk of how their mothers guarded their kitchens with great ferocity from the prying eyes, fingers and appetites of youngsters. Not so in our household. Well, not on Sundays anyway.

As morning moved closer to lunch, I'd tumble off the rocking chair and join Dina to bustle around in our 'professional' aprons with mock authority, rooting through Mum's pots and pans, pretending we knew exactly what we were doing with all her strangely shaped utensils. One of my favourites was Mum's precious old pestle and mortar, the so, so smooth pestle making its fabulous croaking sound whenever it pressed this or that ingredient hard against the mortar. I just loved that noise, and did in fact use it to create my first-ever recipe, herby garlic bread (see page 62).

What heaven it was grinding the rock salt and garlic into a paste. How I loved zesting the lemon (with that funny little gadget thing proper cooks have), then sniffing, whilst snipping the parsley and thyme from the herb garden (I would always hum in what I thought was a really grown-up way whilst doing this chore), before joyfully beating them all into my perfectly soft butter and finally slathering it on to crusty French bread and baking it until crisp on the outside, soft and squidgy on the inside. What joy! Once made, my preferred option was always to slope off and eat it back in Mum's rocking chair. So, if *your* mum hasn't got a rocking chair, add it to the ingredients list on the next page — it's the only way this should be eaten!

Herby Garlic Bread

You may notice that throughout this book I recommend this rather lovely bread just a couple of times …

SERVES 4–6
1 long French baguette
For the herby garlic butter
225g (8oz) best-quality butter
2 tbsp finely chopped fresh lemon thyme
½ tbsp finely chopped fresh rosemary
4 tbsp finely chopped fresh parsley
2–20 garlic cloves, depending on what you have planned
salt and black pepper
finely grated zest and juice of 1 unwaxed lemon

Preheat the oven to 200°C/gas mark 6.

If you don't have a pestle and mortar to pound your butter, herbs and garlic, crush them into a bowl, using a spoon. Season well with salt and pepper and add some lemon zest and juice.

Slice the baguette as thickly as you like, but keep the pieces together so the loaf's shape is intact. Place on a piece of foil large enough to wrap around it later. Now slather each slice on both sides with the deliciously evil butter mixture. If there is any left over, spread it over the crust.

Fold the foil over to make a parcel and pop into the oven for about 20 minutes, or until you can bear it no longer.

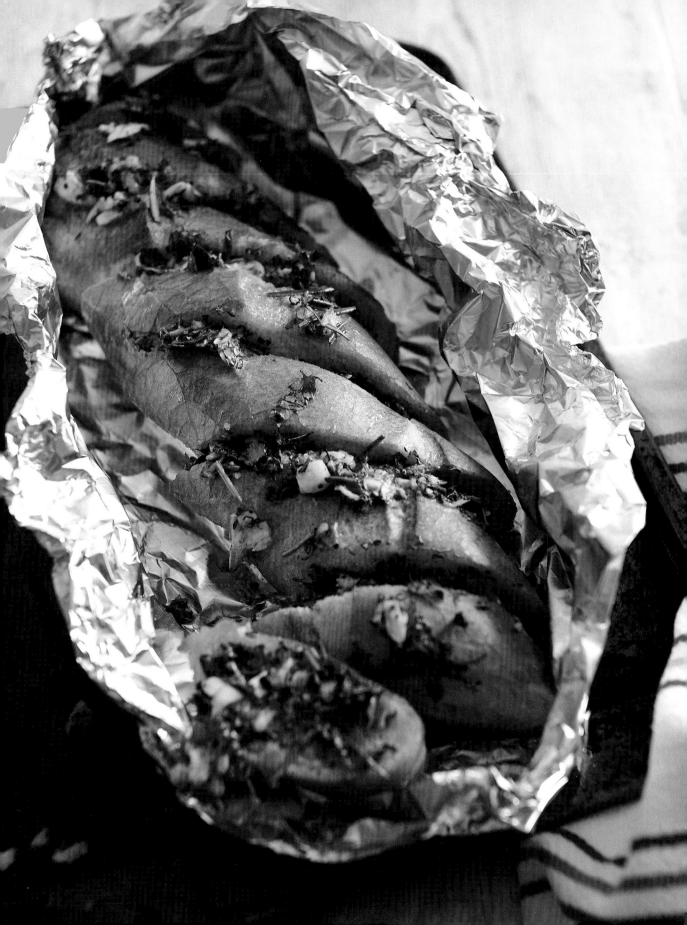

Slow-cooked Spicy Lamb

I reckon Mum could make this dish standing naked on one leg, eyes closed, whistling 'The Star-spangled Banner'. Not just because it's easy, but also because she must have made it more than two hundred times over the years. It was always a favourite, and she could easily make huge dishes of it earlier in the day, or even the day before, especially if they were having a big party, then just heat it up once everyone was ready to feast. If she was serving rice with it, she'd always put a clean tea-towel over it to keep it warm and help it to fluff up.

SERVES 4
sunflower oil
1kg (2¼lb) leg of lamb, cut into 3–4cm (1½in) cubes
1 large onion, peeled and roughly sliced
2 garlic cloves, peeled and chopped
1 tsp baharat spice mix (see page 120)
½ tsp ground cumin
1 tbsp plain flour
400ml (14 fl. oz) lamb or vegetable stock
3 tbsp tomato purée
2 tbsp cumin seeds
fresh coriander, chopped

Heat 4 tbsp oil in a heavy casserole and brown the lamb, a few pieces at a time. Remove to a plate, add the onion and garlic to the pan and cook on a very low heat for 5 minutes. Mix the ground spices into the flour and tip into the pan, still on a low heat and stirring all the time for 2–3 minutes, until you feel the flour is cooked. Add 300ml (½ pint) of the stock and the tomato purée. (You might want to add a bit more stock later if you think the sauce is too thick.)

Fry the cumin seeds in 1 dsp very hot oil in a small frying pan for a few seconds, until they start to jump, then stir them into the stew.

Bring the stew up to a bubble, then turn down to a very low heat and leave to simmer for about 45 minutes, or until the meat is tender. Or (lazy way out) cook in a moderate oven (about 180°C/gas mark 4) for about the same length of time. (I think this is better, because you don't have to keep looking to see if the bottom of the stew is sticking.)

Serve garnished with fresh chopped coriander to taste. My herby garlic bread (see page 62) is great with this dish. (Have you noticed how often I say this?)

My Lentil Dream

This dish is a dream, not only because of its gorgeous flavours but also because it's a dream come true for any host who has both veggie and non-veggie guests. It's a fantastic accompaniment to lamb, chicken or fish, but also works really well with just rice and salad.

SERVES 6–8 AS A SIDE DISH
170g (6oz) brown lentils
4 tbsp olive oil
4 onions, peeled and sliced
1 whole garlic bulb, peeled and crushed
a very large bunch fresh coriander, chopped
1 tsp fine salt
1 heaped tsp each ground cumin and ground allspice
125ml (4 fl. oz) lemon juice
1 tsp pomegranate syrup (from Middle Eastern/Turkish shops
   or large supermarkets)

In a heavy-based saucepan simmer the lentils in 750ml (1¼ pints) water for 20 minutes (no salt yet, as it will toughen the lentils). Remove from the heat, drain and set aside.

Heat 2 tbsp of the oil in a frying pan and fry the onions until they're really nice and brown. Remove with a slotted spoon and put to one side. In the same pan heat the remaining 2 tbsp oil, then throw in the garlic and cook for 1–2 minutes, stirring the whole time. Then add the coriander and stir until it softens.

Add half this mixture and half the onions to the lentils. Now throw in the salt, spices, lemon juice and pomegranate syrup and simmer for a further 20 minutes.

Before you serve this dreamy dish, sprinkle the rest of the coriander and onions over the top.

Dina, praying
at the altar
of roast turkey.

The Big Roast

Cooking in My Grandmother's Footsteps

It's a culinary tragedy that my grandmother's original recipe for her delectable chicken has been lost (quite literally) in the sands of time. But, pluckily (no pun intended), as a family we all plough on, continuing to cook Big Roasts, forever aware of Granny Sawalha sitting on some cloud up above, looking down on us, clucking in disapproval.

I must apologize for blowing my own trumpet. But it's an accepted fact in our households that nobody makes a roast dinner as well as I do, though I must admit it does come at a price.

After any roast dinner in my house the kitchen ends up looking as if a slightly possessed and starving burglar has ransacked it: drawers open, utensils on the floor, vegetable peel in my hair. Put simply, it's carnage.

So what's on the typical roast menu? More often than not I'll roast a couple of gorgeously plump chickens with handfuls of luscious herbs, butter and garlic stuffed under the skin (*à la* dear old Fanny Craddock). On pain of death, there'll be an enormous oven tray filled with the crispiest golden roast potatoes imaginable. Next up is an old family recipe of celery braised in butter and brandy, which is an absolute must (according to every veggie who has passed through my doors), if only for the spectacular aroma with which it fills the kitchen.

Alongside these show-stoppers there's always a supporting cast of carrots steamed in butter, parsley and onion; a tray of sage and sausage stuffing for the chicken, and an apricot, celery and walnut one for the veggies; an extra-terrestrial-sized cauliflower in a creamy cheese and chive sauce is a favourite indulgence for everyone; and though my mother always says it's a 'disgrace' to serve it with chicken, I do a huge, yummy, squidgy, eggy Yorkshire pudding (which, by the way, my mother always, *always* indulges in ...).

As you can probably imagine, it's not until Tuesday of the following week that the kitchen is anywhere near rebuilt and ready to use again.

Sarf London Yorkshire Puds

Before we start, just a few things I've learned from bitter experience about Yorkshire-pudding making:

✸ If you can get good beef dripping to cook the puddings in, I promise the extra flavour is well worth the extra cholesterol.

✸ Don't be impatient when heating the fat (it takes a good 10 minutes), as your little puds simply won't rise unless the fat is hot enough.

✸ If the oil doesn't sizzle when you put in your first spoonful of batter, the oil isn't hot enough, so remove the batter and pop the tin back in the oven. More times than I can remember, my head and heart have told me that the oil has not been hot enough, but my impatient nature has compelled me to carry on, always resulting in disaster.

MAKES 12 PUDDINGS
115g (4oz) plain flour, sifted
½ tsp mixed dried herbs
a pinch salt
2 eggs, beaten
150ml (5 fl. oz) milk
vegetable oil or dripping

Put the flour, herbs and salt in a mixing bowl. Make a well in the middle and add the eggs. Gradually mix in the flour, then slowly stir in the milk and whisk until all lumps have vanished. The batter should be thick enough to coat the back of a spoon. Don't be afraid to add a little more milk if it looks too thick. I usually leave it to rest for about an hour, but often forget and have to use it straight away! It's a good idea to put it into a jug so you can pour it.

Meanwhile, preheat the oven to 220°C/gas mark 7.

When you're ready to cook them, have ready a twelve-hole muffin tin or twelve pudding moulds. Put about 1 tsp oil or, better still, dripping into each mould and then put into the oven until the fat is so hot it's almost smoking. Once it is hot enough, act quickly, pouring in the batter until each mould is almost full, and get them back into the oven as fast as possible.

Cook for 25–30 minutes until risen, puffy and golden.

Don't open the oven too early or your puds might pass out …

Chicken to Die For

My roast chicken is definitely on my last-supper wish list, which is why I'm quite happy to die for it. If I'm honest, I think it's because I do a little bit more than the recipe says. I take a peek every 15 minutes or so, basting my precious bird, maybe turning the garlic cloves over in the juices, adding a little more wine, a bit more seasoning … Basically, a little TLC goes a long way with a roasted bird.

SERVES 4

1 organic chicken, around 1.5–2kg (3¼–4½lb)
lots of nicely softened butter
salt and black pepper
6 garlic cloves, peeled
2 onions, with skin on and halved
2 celery sticks, chopped
1 carrot, peeled and sliced
1 tbsp each fresh parsley and sage (or whatever herbs you prefer)
olive oil
2 good glugs white wine

Preheat the oven to its highest heat.

Rub plenty of butter all over the birdie's skin (a bit more on the breast) and season all over. Put it breast-side down into a roasting tin (I am convinced this allows the juices to run back into the breast. My stepdaughter Issy *loves* this tip and has even introduced it into her own household!) Put the garlic, onion, celery, carrot and herbs around the chicken, and dot with more butter and a really light drizzle of olive oil.

Roast in the middle of the oven for 20 minutes, then take the tray out and turn the chicken over. Lower the temperature to 180°C/gas mark 4 and baste the chicken with the juices. Pour the wine into the bottom of the pan, but not over the chicken, and return to the oven for another 45 minutes, or until the leg juices run clear. (Another way to tell if it's ready is to shake the leg a bit; if it feels loose, it's probably done.)

Leave in the oven to rest, with the door open, for 15 minutes (having turned the oven off, of course), so all those lovely juices run back into the meat.

Perfectly Crisp Roasties

There are few things in life that make me as happy as the sight of piping-hot, perfectly crisp, golden-brown roast potatoes. Every time I make them, Mark proposes (and we've already been married for eight years).

SERVES 6
12 potatoes, peeled and quartered (floury potatoes are best – Maris Piper, Desirée, King Edward)
flaky salt
sunflower oil or duck fat (I know it's very fashionable to use goose fat, but I'm not a fan)

Get the oven nice and hot – about 220°C/gas mark 7.

Pop the potatoes into a saucepan of salty water and bring to the boil, then simmer until just tender. Drain and, if you have time, let them cool. Using a fork, scratch the potatoes all over (this ensures that you get very crisp roasties and is far more effective than just bashing them around in the pan, as some folks do).

Put the oil or fat in a roasting tin in the oven and let it get really hot. It's important that the potatoes aren't too cosy in the pan, or they will steam rather than roast.

Put the potatoes into the hot oil and back into the oven, and cook for about an hour. I do quite a bit of turning and moving of my potatoes throughout, so that every single one of them is totally crisp and golden all over. If you don't have time, don't worry – they'll still be lovely, but it's that extra bit of TLC that makes these babies sublime!

Braised Brandy Celery

I implore you to try this, even if you think you hate celery. It's so good, and a real Sawalha family favourite. The Bovril-and-brandy muddle may sound strange, but it blends into the most unique, delicious flavour. The other great thing about this dish is that if you use Marmite instead of Bovril, it makes fabulous gravy for any vegetarians who might have landed without your noticing.

SERVES 4–6
1 large or 2 small heads celery
300ml (½ pint) vegetable stock
55g (2oz) butter
1 tbsp plain flour
½–1 tsp beef extract (yes, that's Bovril, or veggies can
    use Marmite)
a good slosh brandy or whisky (I usually pour it into
    a wooden spoon and let it splosh over the sides)
salt and plenty of black pepper

Wash the celery and cut the sticks into equal-sized pieces, about 5–7.5cm (2–3in) long. Put in a pan with the stock, bring to the boil and simmer for 15 minutes (or pressure-cook for 1 minute). Drain, reserving the stock.

Melt the butter in a saucepan and brown the flour in it, stirring all the time, until you have a nice nutty aroma. Don't rush this, or the flour will not cook properly and will taste raw. Stir in the stock, beef extract, brandy, salt and pepper, and stir well.

Add the celery and simmer, covered, for about 15 minutes, keeping an eye on it so it doesn't dry out.

Any leftovers can be liquidized, thinned with more stock and – with fresh veg added – this makes a very tasty soup.

Morally Corrupt Carrots
(Not for the Faint-hearted)

My mum, sisters and I always cook our carrots this way if we are having a full-works roast. The extra effort is really worth it for the extra flavour you get.

SERVES 4

500g (1lb 2oz) organic buttery carrots (the nasty taste that
   non-organic carrots can have will absolutely blaze through
   this dish)
25g (1oz) unsalted butter
2 tbsp water
salt
2 tbsp finely chopped onion (but don't be tempted to chop
   it before you're ready to use it, or its flavour will be ruined)
2 tbsp finely chopped fresh parsley (you will probably soon
   be varying these last two ingredients to your own taste)

Peel the carrots (just scrub if they are organic or small and new). Cut into stubby julienne, or leave whole if you are using baby ones.

Put the carrots into a heavy casserole dish with the butter and water, and sprinkle lightly with salt. Cover tightly and simmer on top of the stove for about 45 minutes. Check halfway through cooking to see that the carrots are not burning and keep on checking to see if they're done.

Just before the carrots are done, chop the onion and parsley very finely. As soon as the carrots are ready, add the onion and parsley to the dish and toss for a minute or two.

Sage and Sausage Stuffing

Sometimes, only sometimes, I make a pile of this and eat it all with creamy mash and red wine gravy.

SERVES 4–6
1 large onion, peeled and finely chopped
butter
450g (1lb) good-quality pork sausagemeat
85g (3oz) coarse fresh breadcrumbs
1 tbsp each chopped fresh sage, parsley and thyme
finely grated zest of 1 organic lemon
1 egg, beaten
salt and black pepper

Sauté the onion in a large knob of butter until soft. Remove from the pan and set aside in a mixing bowl to cool. Stir in the sausagemeat, breadcrumbs, herbs, lemon zest and egg, seasoning to taste. Mix together, then form into walnut-sized balls. Place in a roasting tin for 30 minutes until nicely browned.

Apricot, Celery and Walnut Stuffing

This makes a great meat substitute for the vegetarians in the family.

SERVES 4–6
1 medium onion, peeled and finely chopped
4 celery sticks, finely chopped
butter
2 tbsp Calvados
35g (1¼oz) fresh white breadcrumbs
8 dried apricots, soaked for an hour in 2 tbsp boiling water,
    then drained and chopped into small pieces
55g (2oz) shelled walnuts, roughly chopped
salt and black pepper
3 tbsp finely chopped fresh parsley

Gently fry the onion and celery in a large knob of butter until they begin to soften. Pour in the Calvados and let it bubble for 20–30 seconds. Stir in the other ingredients and fry gently for a couple of minutes. Season and stir in the parsley. Put into a greased dish and dot with butter. Bake for 30 minutes at 180°C/gas mark 4.

Pretty Peas à la Franglaise

Mum's version of the French classic involves a lot more than just bringing your peas to the boil and simmering, but it's worth the effort.

SERVES 4–6
55g (2 oz) butter, softened (or more if you are, like me, a butter fiend)
1 round lettuce
a bunch spring onions, roughly chopped
2 lettuce hearts (Little Gem), cut into quarters
500g (1lb 2oz) frozen peas or petits pois (defrosted but still cold)
4 tbsp cold water
caster sugar
salt

Spread a heavy casserole dish thickly with lots of butter, then line it with the outside leaves of the round lettuce. Tie the lettuce quarters with some kitchen string so that they don't fall apart. Arrange around the sides of the pot.

Pour in the peas, scatter the spring onions amongst them and add the water. Hoorah, time for more butter! Add knobs of it all over the top of the peas, then sprinkle with a little sugar and salt to taste. Cover with buttered greaseproof paper and put a lid on the dish. Bring to a gentle boil, simmering for 15 minutes until the lettuce hearts are tender.

Creamy Collie Cheese

Oh, how I love collie cheese and this is a particularly naughty one.

SERVES 4
1 large cauliflower, broken into florets
salt and black pepper
25g (1oz) bacon or pancetta lardons
300ml (½ pint) double cream
115g (4oz) strong Cheddar, grated
40g (1½oz) Parmesan, freshly grated
a large bunch fresh chives, chopped

Season the cauliflower and steam until tender. Put into a warm dish. Dry-fry the lardons, then drain off the fat they've rendered and make them wait!

Gently heat the cream and stir in the cheeses until melted. Drizzle the sauce over the cauliflower and garnish with chopped chives.

Feasts for a Crowd

Bedouins 'n' Breakfast

It's spring and the Sawalhas of South London want lamb. They want it fresh. They want it whole. And they want it cheap. So this means that my father, my cousins Nael, Nayef and Elias, plus half the BBC Arabic Service, will be making a 4 a.m. start at Smithfield meat market in East London.

As kids we loved the theatrics of this annual event. We would all get up half asleep, and clearly half mad, at about 4 a.m. to wave the menfolk off. We'd then put on the mint tea to boil and start making the pitta bread with our mum, all the while waiting to hail the return of our intrepid hunters and, hopefully, an entire spring lamb. I say hopefully, because there was always a frisson of fear that they wouldn't actually come back with anything. Because Smithfield is strictly a retailers-only market, they always ran the risk of being unceremoniously hurled out.

I won't go into the carnage that then ensued, the cultural *faux pas*, the misunderstandings, the hysterical bartering, but when they had managed to pull off their illicit purchase they'd return with the lamb hoisted on their shoulders, crashing into the kitchen, singing, shouting and making ludicrous 'I'm-the-big-brave-hunter' noises. They were like a band of Arab pirates. My sisters and I would be running around, loving the atmosphere, totally over-excited and in awe of this beast that had landed on our kitchen table.

Almost immediately my dad would start carving up the lamb, ready to be squeezed into our minuscule fridge and ice-box (to this day I have no idea how he managed it). My cousins, filled with joy (almost certainly fuelled by the early-morning lager as well as the triumph of 'bringing home the lamb'), would start grilling the kidneys, frying the liver and singing at the top of their voices. My sisters and I would have the job of making the hummus — which, by the way, is the perfect partner for freshly fried liver — whilst my mum would pop the trays of pitta bread into the oven. My job at this point would be to stir the mouhallabieh (my dad's all-time favourite Arabic dessert), a heavenly fragrant rice pudding. In a matter of minutes the table would be groaning under the weight of a feast fit for any dedicated carnivore!

Lebanese Minted Liver

If you don't fancy liver and hummus, try this Lebanese recipe, which is so easy to make and has a really unique flavour. The original doesn't use wine: if you prefer you can replace it with vinegar. Be really careful not to overcook the liver, because it will absolutely ruin the dish.

SERVES 4–6
450g (1lb) liver (I prefer calf's, but use whatever
    you fancy), sliced
salt and black pepper
1 dsp olive oil
25g (1oz) butter
1 onion, peeled and thinly sliced
2 garlic cloves, peeled and chopped
125ml (4 fl. oz) white wine, or white wine vinegar
1½ tsp plain flour
1 tbsp dried mint, crushed
3–4 tbsp cold water
fresh coriander, chopped

Season the liver with salt and black pepper. Heat the oil, in a heavy-based frying pan, then drop in most of the butter. Once melted, flash-fry the liver on both sides, remove from the pan and put to one side. Add a little more butter if it looks as if it needs it, then fry the onion and garlic until soft. Now pour in the wine and let the alcohol burn off a little. Add the flour and stir for a minute or so, then add the mint and water, and let it bubble for a few minutes.

Pop the liver back into the sauce and if it needs it add a little more water. Let it simmer for a few minutes until the liver is just cooked. I like my liver pink; others prefer it cooked through. Pierce with a sharp knife and have a peek. Sprinkle with a little freshly chopped coriander.

A Party Fit for a King

Uncle Nabil, Dad's youngest brother, is irrefutably the life and soul of the party: outrageous, charming, opinionated, talented and egotistical. When I was a child, he was my very favourite uncle in the entire world. A trip to Jordan always meant we would stay at his fabulously glamorous house in uptown Amman, where he lived with his young son Ziad. An actor and comedian, Nabil is so incredibly famous in the Middle East that he quite literally cannot walk down the street. To get a grasp of his popularity, think Peter Sellers of the Arab world and you're some way to realizing how famous he is in Jordan.

But one of the best things about staying at Uncle Nabil's was that we got to go to all the incredibly glamorous parties he constantly threw: the best one ever being the one attended by King Hussein of Jordan. Yes! A *reeeeeeaal* king! When my sisters and I were told the news we were so excited I was worried one of us might pass out there and then.

The King's acceptance of his invitation came on the morning of the actual party and within the hour the house was swarming with secret police. They went into every room, and even up on to the roof. They checked the verandas, the gardens, the garage and every last thing in the kitchen. The best bit was when they pulled out bottles of Milton fluid (the sterilizing fluid for babies' bottles) and insisted that all the fruits and vegetables were washed in it ...

Everything was so exciting not only because of the secret police but also because, the minute we heard that the King was coming, all the party preparations suddenly shot up a level. This was now going to be a P-AAA-RTY!

From that moment Uncle Nabil seemed to have the phone surgically attached to his ear, ordering extra furniture by the truckload, calling in favours to secure the best entertainers, all the while berating the army of people who were running back and forth setting up thousands of fairy lights, polishing, sweeping and scrubbing every inch of the house. In each room we went into the excitement was ever more palpable, and none more so than in the kitchen. As my sisters and I stole into the culinary HQ, our eyes like saucers, we were instantly hit by the familiar assault on the senses that you always get when you enter an Arab kitchen in full action.

The kitchen was fit to burst with more than three times as many people as usual. Even men had been allowed in and were busily cooking a huge mansaf, whilst the women were preparing dozens and dozens of meze dishes. The atmosphere was at fever pitch when suddenly Nabil, his phone still plastered to his ear, swept in, followed by the local butcher's son with a whole lamb (dead, of course) balanced on his shoulder. My heart leapt! I knew what this meant, and of course it was the perfect dish to serve to a King. It was … (drum roll) … Uncle Nabil's stuffed lamb – a truly delicious feast of a dish, where the lamb is stuffed with an abundance of pistachios, walnuts, raisins, almonds, masses of spices and saffron rice. It's then stitched up tightly and, wait for it, roasted for hours on charcoal, creating the most out-of-this-world dish you could imagine – and believe me, my brilliant uncle makes the best there is.

I suppose the punchline to this story is that the King did indeed come to the party and he was absolutely the most polite, entertaining and charming of men (he even gave an official royal decree to Julia that she was not allowed to sunbathe, as my mum had snitched and told him that she was sunburnt but refused to stay out of the sun). But unfortunately, the one thing he decidedly wasn't was hungry! Can you believe that by the time he left (having had a fabulous time), not a single morsel had passed his lips. Now, in my book, royal or not, that was just plain weird. To this day, a tiny part of me wonders whether the secret police were slightly concerned that the Milton fluid just wasn't quite reliable enough …

✦ ✧ ✦ ✧ ✦ ✧ ✦ ✧ ✦

Uncle Nabil's Desert-baked Whole Lamb

If you have between fifteen and twenty hungry people in your life, this lamb will feed them all. If you feel squeamish, you could get your butcher to bone it for you …

Because the traditional way of cooking this dish involves digging a pit in the desert, building a fire in it and then cooking the wrapped lamb for 4–5 hours, buried under piles of sand, I thought I'd adapt the recipe a little for you! But, if you'd like to try to re-create the desert in your own back yard (as my nutty family does in deepest South London), I will share with you how …

First dig a pit (not your average recipe instruction) about 1 metre (3 feet) deep and, depending on the length of your lamb, roughly 60 x 150cm (2 x 5 feet). If the earth is damp, put a layer of bricks or stones in the bottom, then create a deep bed of charcoal and wood. Light the fire, then wait until the coals are white. Wrap your stuffed meat in foil, pop it in the fire, then cover it with soil (or sand). The lamb will take a good 4–5 hours to cook and will be meltingly soft, easily falling from the bones.

SERVES 15–20
6.75kg (15lb) whole lamb
juice of 4 lemons
olive oil
salt and black pepper
For the stuffing
900g (2lb) long-grain rice, thoroughly washed and drained
3 onions, peeled and chopped
5 tbsp olive oil
½ tbsp each ground ginger, ground cinnamon, ground
  allspice and cardamom seeds
300g (10½oz) whole pistachio nuts
300g (10½oz) walnuts, chopped
300g (10½oz) fried whole almonds
225g (8oz) raisins
5 tsp salt
3 tsp freshly ground black pepper

Preheat the oven to 180°C/gas mark 4.

Measure your oven before you order the lamb so that you can give your butcher the exact size! It does help if you have a *big* oven. If doing it outside, get the shortest member of the family to lie on the ground and draw a rectangle around them. Just make sure they get up, you don't want to cook them!

To prepare the stuffing, first cook the rice in water to cover, making sure you season it well, for about 20 minutes.

Fry the onions in the oil until soft, then add all the spices and stir until they begin to release their aroma. Add the rice, nuts, raisins, salt and pepper. Put to one side.

With a damp cloth, wipe the lamb inside and out, then rub the lemon juice into the cavity and skin. Press the rice mixture inside the lamb and sew up the opening with a trussing needle and kitchen twine. Tie the feet together as tightly as possible. Rub olive oil, salt and black pepper all over the skin. Now wrap and seal the lamb loosely in foil.

Haul into the oven and cook for about 2 hours. Take the foil off for the last 45 minutes and continue cooking until the meat is very tender and nicely browned. Nabil always turns it over at least once, but it is quite a performance and extraordinarily messy!

When you're happy with it, lift it out on to a large serving dish. Cut the thread and spoon out some of the stuffing. We usually garnish our little lamb with plenty of parsley and sliced tomatoes.

Mark and Uncle Nabil filming the desert-baked lamb in Jordan.

The Party of a Lifetime

One of the best parties I've ever been to in my life was slap-bang in the middle of the Sahara Desert in Morocco. I was in Warzarzat (a dusty desert town), playing the part of an Arabian princess, Ankh, in my first ever film, *Slave of Dreams*.

My first day on set had been an absolute whirlwind — meeting the other actors, being fussed over by costume and make-up designers and, of course, lapping up the whole glamorous world of LA movie-making. As far as I was concerned, I'd stepped straight into a dream I'd been having since I was a little girl. Having travelled with my father to *his* movie sets all over the world, I had finally arrived at *my own*.

Unbeknownst to me, however, the truly indulgent part of this Hollywood experience had nothing to do with anything going on in front of the camera. By the time I arrived, the cast and crew had already spent three months slogging it out in the desert — so I walked into a well-oiled machine of camera operators, sound recordists, gaffers, etc., all of whom by now were suffering profound homesickness. To cheer themselves up, they had decided to throw the party to end all parties. And, being a truly international production, their culinary suffering was about to become a foodie heaven.

Every nation that was represented in the film crew did its bit. Believe it or not, the Italians, precisely in preparation for such an occasion, had spent weeks growing emergency basil on their hotel balconies, and once the green light for a celebration had been given, immediately placed orders for fresh fish, pasta, buffalo mozzarella and pizza flour, all to be flown in directly from Rome.

The indigenous Moroccans had brought an abundance of sumptuous silks, rugs and pillows to dress the party 'set'. They had also cajoled their mothers, sisters and grannies into supplying tagines filled with succulent meats and fruits so that their new-found friends in the film industry could experience an authentic taste of Morocco.

Not surprisingly, the Brits, bless them, had successfully organized the delivery of copious amounts of booze and (maybe more surprisingly) set up all the fairy lights to twinkle away with the millions of stars that come out to play in the midnight desert sky.

The Americans were, of course, supplying the biggest, meanest, juiciest burgers, specially flown in from the States. Even the pickles came by FedEx. In true Yankee fashion, they had also ventured up into the mountains and hired a troop of Berber drummers and belly-dancers to ensure the party would keep jumping until the small hours.

In a remarkable show of industry, the carpenters had constructed for one night, and one night only, an amazing open-air restaurant, complete with wood-fired oven in preparation for some delicious Napoli pizzas that would be baked for everyone by the opera-singing director of photography.

So, once the director had called a wrap on my first day's filming, I was to be blown away by my first experience of feature-film catering on the set of my first film! Although I'd been playing a fictional princess all day, the after-shoot party, with all its colours, smells, flavours, tastes and aromas, was infinitely more regal and luxurious than anything we'd shot!

One particular dish stood out for me: a gorgeously sweet, succulent lamb and date tagine. The mother and sister of the on-set translator Mohammed had lovingly prepared it, and the next day, after seeing how enthusiastically I ate it, he offered to take me to his mother Fewzia's house for a lesson in authentic Moroccan cuisine. What an absolute treat! I spent the most glorious afternoon with these incredibly skilled women, looking and learning. Although we didn't speak a word of each other's language we managed to communicate brilliantly with plenty of miming and gurning. And when the heat of the day lifted, we ate out on their terrace under the stars. It had been quite simply a perfect day.

Spiced Lamb and Date Tagine

Of course it is fabulous to make this recipe in a traditional tagine dish, not only because it looks great but also because I think it tastes better too. Don't worry too much, though, if you don't have one — just use a heavy-based pan instead. (If you *are* using a tagine dish, you will need to put a heat diffuser underneath it or it will crack!)

SERVES 4

1kg (2¼lb) leg of lamb
a dollop butter
2 tbsp olive oil
1 medium onion, peeled and thinly sliced
2 tsp each ground cinnamon and ground ginger
500ml (18 fl. oz) water
3 tbsp chopped dates
salt and black pepper
2 tbsp runny honey
2 tbsp lemon juice
To serve
8 fresh dates, stoned
55g (2oz) whole shelled almonds, toasted
1 tbsp sesame seeds, toasted

Get your butcher to cut the lamb into even cubes about 14cm (1½in). Melt the butter and oil together in a tagine or heavy-based pan and seal the meat on all sides. Add the onions and cook them really, really slowly until translucent. Now you can add those heady spices and stir them until their aroma is released.

Pour in the water and drop in the chopped dates. Season well, then cover and cook really slowly until the meat is as soft as butter: 1—1½ hours. The most heavenly aromas will fill your home!

To finish, stir in the honey and lemon juice. Lastly, scatter on the fresh dates, then sprinkle on the toasted almonds and sesame seeds. Make sure you have plenty of bread to mop up the delicious sauce.

Laughing in the Face of Recipes

My lovely cousin Laurice (aka my father's niece, Auntie Jamileh's daughter, Cousin Elias's wife, and one of my very favourite relatives) has always had a heart of gold, but she also has a very wicked sense of humour and a very dangerous giggle to go with it.

I say 'dangerous' for a reason, because, when it starts, not only does it slowly infect everyone in her immediate vicinity but, like a self-generating battery, she continuously re-charges herself so that, once she starts laughing, an upwards spiral occurs, gathering height, speed, dizziness and danger. A hum of hysteria grows around her and, within seconds (like a pan of exploding popcorn), she's got everyone in the room popping with laughter. What it's about is never clear, but it never really matters: Laurice's laughter is always much funnier than whatever originally caused it.

As ever, food also plays a huge part in any merriment, for Laurice is a great home cook and is passionate about traditional Arabic food. One of her specialities is kibbeh, a very popular dish in the Middle East. There are many variations, moving from the relatively easy (the recipe I'm sharing with you) to the very tricky (which, in the Arab world, is widely regarded as needing the '*special* kibbeh finger' to pull off perfectly).

Kibbeh can be eaten raw, fried or baked and is made from burghul wheat, lamb, spices and pine nuts. Until quite recently I had never actually made it, though over the years I've naturally devoured it countless times. And, whenever the opportunity arises, I still do. So, let's jump-cut to a family wedding, gathering steam in the beautiful Hampshire countryside on a hot summer's day in 2009. Laurice's gorgeous daughter Tanoushka has fallen in love with her lovely Joe and, after a whirlwind romance, is rather joyously (and quite quickly) pregnant.

Blimey, you're thinking, what's this got to do with kibbeh? Well, Laurice, being as big-hearted as she is, decided that she'd make *all* the food for all 150 guests! Naturally, as a family we couldn't stand back and not help. No, we rolled up our sleeves and got stuck in.

My contribution was mussakhan wraps and spicy meatballs, but I was also very keen to help with the kibbeh – not an entirely altruistic act, as I've always wanted to learn how to make it properly. So, the week before the big day, with my mother beside me armed with pad and paper, we headed down to Laurice and Elias's place, eager to record every detail of how to make the perfect kibbeh.

As soon as Laurice answered the door she burst out laughing. Sure enough, Mum and I found ourselves following suit, totally oblivious as to why, and were quickly in absolute agony, cackling like hyenas on her doorstep. Some time into this hysteria, Laurice managed to explain, in between snorts, that when she saw us clutching our stationery she thought it hilarious that we were planning to write down the recipe. It wasn't long before we found out why it had tickled her so much.

As is the way with most great Middle Eastern cooks, Laurice doesn't weigh or measure a single solitary ingredient. She simply knows, by instinct, how much of everything she needs in order to hit perfection. It's what I call 'culinary DNA'.

So, after a fabulous morning spent cooking, gossiping and, of course, incessantly giggling, Mum and I left the house with a detailed method for the recipe – but, as Laurice doesn't even own a pair of scales, we had absolutely no measurements whatsoever. But don't worry, Mum and I have made this at least six times since, using our scales, in order to bring you a perfect recipe.

Just like the stirring, it's absolutely vital that you constantly laugh throughout the making of this dish. Your family and friends will think you're mad, but they'll shut up when they taste your kibbeh …

Kibbeh – a Cracking Lamb Dish
(Minced Lamb with Cracked Wheat)

Kibbeh is a mixture of burghul wheat, spiced lamb and onions, which is pounded to a paste (don't worry, you can use a food processor), spread into a baking tray and then filled with lamb, onions and pine nuts before another layer of kibbeh is placed on top. Imagine a sandwich with the kibbeh mixture as the bread and the meat and pine nuts as the filling.

SERVES 4–6 AS A MAIN COURSE
butter
olive oil
whole shelled almonds
For the filling
1 medium onion, peeled and finely chopped
450g (1lb) minced lamb
1 tsp baharat spice mix (see page 120)
salt and lots of black pepper
a handful pine nuts, fried in a little olive oil
For the kibbeh
350g (12oz) burghul (cracked wheat), washed and drained
450g (1lb) minced lamb (fatty is best)
1 medium onion, peeled and finely chopped
1 tsp salt
2 tsp each ground allspice and ground cinnamon

Preheat the oven to 200°C/gas mark 6. You will need a heavily buttered oven tray 40 x 50cm (16 x 20in).

For the filling, fry the onion in 85g (3oz) of the butter and 1 tbsp of the oil until soft. Stir in the meat, spice, salt and pepper. Simmer for 5 minutes or so. Add the pine nuts and put to one side.

For the kibbeh, first get rid of all the excess water from the burghul (Laurice puts it in a sieve and then presses down to squeeze out every last drop). Next, put the lamb and onion in a food processor and whizz a couple of times. Now take it out, wet your hands with cold water and knead the mixture with the burghul (do this quite vigorously). Pop it all back in the processor and whizz again. Take it back out (it's a bit of a palaver, isn't it?) and with wet hands knead in the salt and spices.

When everything is really soft (paste-like) and well mixed, divide the kibbeh mixture into eight equal-sized balls. Now wet your hands and flatten four of the balls, one by one, between your palms. Put them into the buttered oven tray. Again with cold wet hands, flatten it all out, making sure there are no holes and that it is even. Spread the filling all over the top of this, then cover with the other four balls of kibbeh in the same way as before. Now run a knife all round the edge and cut into diamond shapes, then put a whole almond on each piece.

Melt about 55g (2oz) butter with 1–2 tbsp oil and pour all over the top. Bake for 30–45 minutes until brown and crisp. You can eat this hot or cold with yogurt and a mixed salad.

My goddess-like cousin Tanoushka and her lovely hubby Joe.

The Mansaf Party

The mansaf! No, not some horrific monster from *1001 Arabian Nights*.
But neither is it simply a dish or a recipe. No, the mansaf is an event,
a scene from a film, a dramatic and theatrical moment in the fabric
of family life. Mansaf is a traditional and celebratory Jordanian meal.
In other words, it's the cheapest and easiest way to feed a whole lot of
people in one go with no plates, knives or forks, and yet it makes them
feel as though they've been royally treated and well stuffed. It's enjoyed
at weddings, but more often after funerals for family members, as
the family of the dead never eat before the burial. So you can imagine
the unspoken words, 'Thank God he's gone – now we can have a
good stuffing.'

Let me paint the scene … My dad's in the loft, hurling down bales of
fabric in stunning reds, deep pinks and oranges to a couple of my surly
teenage cousins. My mum is in the kitchen, whisking egg whites for
one of her divine pavlovas. My sisters and I are chopping huge bunches
of rich green parsley and coriander, whilst alternately giggling and
bickering. Aunties and cousins, puffed up with importance, sit rolling
piles of vine leaves. On the stove there's an enormous saucepan of
apricots and raisins, simmering in their own juices, fragrant with
cinnamon sticks, cloves, vanilla.

My cousin Nayef barks out orders to anyone he thinks is not
pulling their weight: 'Mazin! Do you think the carrots will peel
themselves? Leila! Stop eating the sugared almonds, we have people
coming, for God's sake. Youssef! What are those spots on your face?
People are coming at seven. See what you can do … Nadia, you've
put on weight since last week …'

The din is earsplitting, the grown-ups are stressed and we're in
our element. We're having a party! Our typically English dining room
in Upper Norwood (just 2 miles from Croydon) would be magically
transformed into an authentic Bedouin tent, dressed with dozens of
twinkling lanterns, huge pillows scattered on the floor to encourage
lounging and gorging, and the reflections of candlelight glittering in
the Sellotape used to stick my father's bales of fabric to the walls …

Dishes of shiny black olives, lovingly marinated in garlic and thyme, placed on circular hammered-copper tables, silver bowls of pickled turnips, radishes and mild green chillies to nibble on whilst waiting for the main event: the mansaf!

Dad worshipping at the temple of Mansaf.

Mansaf is my mother's most loathed dish next to melokhia. It is made up of big chunks of lamb cooked in yogurt and spices, served on a mountain of rice and fried nuts, all on a dish that's a metre (3 feet) in diameter, needing two very strong men to carry it.

As a child I absolutely loved watching the faces of European guests at the moment the mansaf was brought ceremoniously into the light. There would be great gasps of wonder — and fear (there's always fear in a mansaf crowd), as none of them had ever seen anything quite like it before. This was always a moment of great pride for me, as I was sure there was no other family on the planet as exotic and as generous as mine.

More often than not, after the mansaf would come the belly-dancing. I'd shamelessly show off, thinking I was the bee's knees. The only thing that would bring me to a halt were my mother's desserts.

Whether it was her out-of-this-world creamy lemon soufflé with dainty *langue du chat* biscuits, her pavlova with its perfect marshmallowy middle, or her pear tart with the most delectable rich almond pastry — they were all calling me and, like a hypnotized snake, I would shake my belly in their general direction.

After all the excitement, and empty plates, I'd fall into a stupor on the silken cushions, sleepily watching the party play on, dreaming of the leftovers I might find in the morning …

That's me in the middle in the funky pants.

Honour Thy Guests — Mansaf
(A Mountain of Lamb, Rice and Yogurt)

For this recipe, I'm afraid I am handing you over to my Uncle Nabil, as he is indisputably the mansaf king in our family.

SERVES ABOUT 6–10
1.5kg (3lb 5oz) young lamb (legs, ribs or shoulder with bone),
   cut into lady's-fist-size chunks
2 large onions, peeled and sliced
salt and black pepper
2 small cinnamon sticks
1½ tsp ground turmeric
2 tsp ground allspice
vegetable oil
85g (3oz) rice per person (real rice – none of that sissy, tasteless
   basmati nonsense, but good cooking Egyptian or round rice)
very thin, large pitta breads (see page 136), split in halves, or,
   better still, wraps
6 tbsp pine nuts
For the yogurt sauce
600ml (1 pint) natural yogurt
1 egg white
2 tsp cornflour

THE COOKING

Thoroughly wash the lamb, put it in a large pan, cover with cold water and bring to the boil, skimming well. Meanwhile, gently fry the onion and the spices, including the salt and pepper, in a little oil.

Once the meat liquid is boiling, add the fried onion and spices, which will ensure that the lamb smell does not chase you out into the street or, worse, the street chase you out of the area. Cover and cook for about an hour. The meat must be well cooked and tender, easy to pull off the bone with one hand but not so cooked that it falls off the bone itself. Remove the lid and reduce the liquid until it just covers the lamb. Cook the rice as usual.

Traditionally, *marees* or *sharab* (a specially made yogurt, drained of water, salted and left to dry to hard balls in the sun) would have already been prepared by cracking the yogurt balls into small chunks, soaking them in warm water and blending into a slightly thick sauce. In the absence of yogurt balls, use the ingredients listed above.

Place the yogurt in a heavy pan. Beat the egg white until frothy and blend it into the yogurt with the cornflour. Bring slowly to the boil, stirring constantly, then lower the heat and simmer uncovered until it begins to thicken.

Drain the meat of 90 per cent of its juice, reserving the juice. Add the yogurt sauce to the pan, bring to the boil and simmer for 5–10 minutes.

Fry the pine nuts in a generous dose of oil, but keep stirring them until they're a nice golden colour and do *not* burn them.

THE SERVING AND STUFFING

Now get a big tray and arrange the pitta bread over it. Pour the rice from its pot into the middle of the tray and spread it into a pyramid, then take the meat chunks out of the pot and evenly and gently arrange them on the pile of rice. Spread the pine nuts all over, but mainly round the edges. Pour the yogurt sauce into a glass bowl and, using a ladle, pour the sauce round the outer edge of the tray, in front of the guests but not on their hands or toes — the sauce is hot. Now with your head high and your best stage voice, say, '*Tfadalu*' (dig in).

As a host you keep your eye on the guest who might need more sauce and does not have enough meat in front of him. Even though the other greedy guests may have devoured their share, they will be the first to destroy your mansaf reputation if they're not stuffed to an eye-popping degree. '*Sahtain*' (good health)!

THE EATING PROTOCOL

A tray of mansaf usually feeds around ten people (though there have been trays big enough to take fifty-plus stuffers), standing at 45°, eating with one hand, which is brought down into the rice-and-meat pile like a dive bomber. It is then pulled out with a mixture of bread, rice and meat, the mixture is skilfully rolled into a ball and flicked into the mouth with the thumb. (Flicking your ball into somebody else's mouth is a sign of endearment.) By the way, the other hand is kept behind you, ready for a sudden urge to scratch.

It has been found that when eating by hand you consume twice as much food. So the knife and fork, which were invented by the Arabs in Spain, was a form of dieting.

You practically never have to wash the 80cm (32in) wide tray the food was served on. Happy mansaf!

The Road to Ramallah

Before they married, my mother was my father's secretary in the BBC Arabic Service at that very imposing and most highly regarded of Auntie's buildings, Bush House on The Strand. Back in those days when you worked in the Overseas Service, as they did, the 'foreigners' in the department would get annual home leave. And so when Dad went back off to Jordan, my mother (now a little bit more than his secretary) would naturally join him.

By all accounts, it was on one of these trips that my father's brother-in-law, Uncle Zaki, told them both about an incredible dish he had discovered in a restaurant in the heart of Ramallah. Not understanding a word that was being said, Mum didn't quite catch the name of the dish before she found herself in a car, rattling along a dirt-track road towards … Ramallah.

When they arrived, Mum says the so-called 'restaurant' was really more of a makeshift garage, painted a lurid green with blindingly bright striplights tied to its ceiling and just three rickety tables.

Even though it had been a 2-hour, boneshaking, whiplash-inducing drive from Amman to this Palestinian 'paradise', my parents were so smitten with the new-found delicacy that they made this culinary pilgrimage eight more times in their two-week holiday. So, what was this holy grail of a meal that was such a unifying force in my parents' relationship? Well, just as they'd fallen in love with each other, they'd also fallen in love with the Great Mussakhan.

I think the entire family would say it is one of their all-time favourite Arabic dishes. How could it not be, with the plumpest, juiciest chicken roasted with berry-red sumac, piles of fried onions layered over the chicken, wafer-thin shrak bread lying beneath, collecting the intensely flavoured naughty juices, making it, yes, hideously fattening, but also utterly, utterly heavenly.

I am drooling as I write. This really is a 'must-try' recipe, not just because it tastes gorgeous but because it looks fabulous too, the sumac giving the dish a beautiful winey-red colour that contrasts so well with the pyramid of snow-white basmati rice scattered with glistening trails of butter, roasted almonds and pine nuts.

Mussakhan
(Roasted Chicken on a Magical Carpet of Bread, Onions and Sumac)

I think this dish is one of those that, if given a bit of extra love and attention, can go from being simply delicious to simply divine. I ensure this by standing over the onions the entire time they're cooking, stirring, tasting and adjusting the seasoning to get not only the *taste* perfect but also the *texture*. Needless to say, I'm often full by the time we sit down to eat it!

SERVES 4
8 chicken pieces, dried with a kitchen towel
2 tbsp vegetable oil
shrak bread (a very thin Arabic bread; from Middle Eastern
   shops) preferably, or tortilla wraps or even pitta bread
For the onion mixture
6–8 good glugs olive oil
8 large onions, sliced
125ml (4 fl. oz) chicken stock
a pinch caster sugar
8–10 tbsp sumac (from Middle Eastern shops)

First make the onion mixture that goes over the roasted chicken. You can do this the day before if you like, and marinate the chicken pieces with it. Heat the olive oil in a very large frying pan, then throw in the onions. Salt them and cook them really slowly; this should take 20–25 minutes. You can give them the occasional stir, or the big love treatment as above. Once they're glisteningly soft, add the stock, stir and allow to bubble a little, then add the sugar and stir again … and again … and again. Add the beauteous, berry-red sumac and, you've guessed it … stir!

Meanwhile, preheat the oven to 180°C/gas mark 4.

Brown the chicken pieces in the vegetable oil.

Line the tin with a couple of layers of shrak bread and half the onion mixture. Lay the chicken on top of this and cover with the rest of the onion mixture. If you have time, leave to marinate again. Put it all back in the oven and cook for another 20–25 minutes, or until the chicken is cooked through.

Make sure everyone gets some of the bread, even if they think they don't want it — it tastes unbelievably good. Serve with steamed rice garnished with fried pine nuts and almonds, a bowl of creamy yogurt and a green salad.

The Kafarty King Is Back in Town

Hooray! My cousin Nayef and his family are flying into London from their home in Saudi Arabia. Which means a whole string of family parties is imminent. In particular, Nayef's legendary kafarty parties!

As kids, we'd literally do laps of honour around the garden, screaming, 'It's kafarty party time' again and again, until Mum would hurl a copper pan at us.

What the hell is 'karfarty', you ask? Well, the *correct* name for these sinfully good Arabic pancakes is kataef, but as a toddler Dina couldn't pronounce this, so ever since these little delicacies have been referred to as 'kafarties'.

Traditionally they're a wedding dessert, and are served warm, with sweet, rose-scented syrup, sugared nuts and clotted (yes, clotted) cream. As far as Nayef (and the rest of us actually) is concerned, these little beauties are delicious enough to warrant wedding parties held solely in their own honour, with no need whatsoever for a bride. 'I tell you,' he would exclaim, in his unique transatlantic Jordanian-American drawl, 'given the choice, I would rather marry a kafarty. Imagine that! A kafarty bride *and* kafarty to celebrate!'

Nayef (as you've probably gathered) is a larger-than-life character, who went on to set up the clothes firm Bench and Hooch, though it would have been no surprise if his clothes firm had actually been called kafarty! Anyway, Nayef was indisputably the kafarty-making king, not only because he's a fabulous cook but also because he's a fabulous showman.

He would come directly from Heathrow to our kitchen, immediately filling it with his enormous personality as he rolled up his sleeves ready to cook. 'Everyone! Clear some space. I'm here. The king is back in town!'

He was also king of the put-downs, and he'd start dishing out insults even before dishing out pancakes.

'Nadia, I bought you some delicious chocolates from the plane. I'm sure you would like some, even though your bottom is begging you not to eat them!'

These were always greeted with nervous peals of laughter from my sisters and from his children, Mazin, Leila and Ingrid. Nervous, because no one really knew who would be next.

'My God, Julia! You are really growing up. How many spots do you have now? Do the boys hide from you at school?'

A little bit like Russian roulette, the longer it took him to get to you, the more nervous you became …

'My God, we need more cream. But that's lucky for you, Dina, heh? You could do with the exercise, darling.'

These would all be fired out at speed whilst he simultaneously measured, whisked and fried. No one would be spared from his mickey-taking as he flipped one pancake after another.

'Haraam [poor thing]! You are so busy, Bobby [directed at my mother]. I know this because I can see you didn't have time to hoover the house or prepare your hair.'

His volley of put-downs was a bit like those scenes from *Bugsy Malone*, when they shoot cakes at everyone instead of bullets. He is almost Tourette's-like in his compulsion to say the most outrageous things, and yet, whenever he's fired a shot, there is always a stunned silence before he starts with his incredibly contagious giggle. And so, once *he* started laughing, *we* would all follow suit. I've witnessed this pattern time and time again and am always in awe at how he's got away with it for all these years without getting a black eye.

Though in matter of fact, it is Nayef's way of softening people up. If he feels you can take a good ribbing, he'll become your most loyal friend and supporter, and the big bonus is that Nayef will then naturally (at some point) make you some kafarties, declaring at the top of his voice, 'It's kafarty party time! The Kafarty King is back in town!'

Kataef *(Arabic Pancakes - aka Kafarties)*

Now although at first glance this does appear to be quite a fiddly recipe, it's actually quite easy — so go on, have a go. Treat everyone — they will taste the love, I promise!

MAKES 16-20

For the rose-scented syrup
400ml (14 fl. oz) water
550g (1¼lb) caster sugar
1 tbsp lemon juice
2 tbsp rosewater

For the batter
2 tsp dried yeast
4 tsp warm water
3 tsp caster sugar
250g (9oz) plain flour
3 tsp baking powder
500ml (18 fl. oz) water
1 tsp rosewater (optional)

For the sweet nuts
280g (10oz) shelled walnuts
4 tbsp icing sugar
4 tsp ground cinnamon

To cook and serve
vegetable oil
clotted cream

To make the syrup, pour the water, sugar and lemon juice into a heavy-bottomed pan. Bring it up to a bubble, then turn down the heat and simmer for 10 minutes. Stir in the rosewater, then pop it in the fridge for later.

For the batter, put the yeast and warm water in a small bowl. Stir in the sugar and leave it in a warm place for about 10 minutes or until it bubbles. Sift the flour and baking powder into a bowl and then gradually add the water and the yeast mixture. Keep whisking — no lumps wanted! Add the rosewater if you fancy. Now cover the mixture and leave it for 1½ hours to rise.

For the sweet nuts, simply chop the walnuts roughly and stir in the icing sugar and cinnamon.

When the batter has risen, grease a non-stick frying pan with a very thin layer of oil (you'll need to do this between each pancake). Heat it over a medium heat until it's very hot, then bring the heat down a bit. Pour a large

spoonful of the batter into the pan and tilt it to spread it out — but only a little bit: you want a nice round shape and thickness a bit like an American pancake. Once the pancake starts to bubble, flip it over and fry the other side.

To serve, sprinkle a spoonful of nuts on each kafarty, with a dollop of clotted cream and then a swirl of syrup. Divine!

Nayef claiming his cook's perks!

In keeping with family tradition — not a single face is fully visible!

A Thousand and One
Arabian Bites

Feasting in Jericho

As children holidaying in Jordan, my sisters and I adored going to Abu Ahmed's. No, not some eccentric uncle, but rather a glorious garden-restaurant deep in the city of Jericho. Honestly, this place had to be seen to be believed. It was vast and completely overrun with the most flamboyantly scarlet poinsettia bushes the size of trees.

The cacophony of sounds created by both the intense chattering of diners and the twittering of birds high up in the trees was strangely melodic. It was *so* exciting for us girls, the smoke from the barbecues and the wonderful muggy odour of cigars only intensifying the gloriously exotic foreign-ness of it all. Spread across the floor were these fabulous Aladdin-like rugs and throws. The whole place felt as if it were about to take off from the pages of *1001 Arabian Nights*.

The speciality of the house was a spectacularly theatrical meze. Once ordered, within minutes a feast of up to a hundred small dishes would begin, served over a period of several hours.

The to-ing and fro-ing of dishes, going back and forth, here and there, was hypnotizing: no sooner was one dish finished than another magically appeared in its place. There were entire fictional worlds of divine delicacies on these little plates: juicy barbecued meats; deep-fried savoury pastries; dangerously more-ish dips made of courgettes, aubergines, sometimes walnuts; succulent cuts of meat; spicy sausages; baskets of out-of-this-world freshly baked breads; and the most sumptuous array of curious-looking salads.

With our tummies fit to burst, my sisters and I would lie on the big squashy cushions and delight in watching my father and his friends smoking their hubbly-bubblies whilst getting gently sozzled on aniseed-flavoured arak, all the while regaling each other with endless stories from their childhoods. Lying there on the plush pillows, playing with all the magical tassels hanging from them, I would drift on my imaginary magic carpet above the debris of the table, floating off to a land far, far away — a land that to adults is affectionately known as 'Foodie Coma'.

Here are just some of the tasty dishes that managed to induce a stuffed loss of consciousness in my sisters and me.

Sambousek (Spinach Kisses)

This recipe will make loads of pastries — but none of them will ever make it to the freezer!

MAKES 30–40 PASTRIES
For the dough
10g (¼oz) dried yeast
a pinch caster sugar
300ml (½ pint) warm water
500g (1¼lb) strong white bread flour
1 tbsp fine salt
6 tbsp olive oil
melted butter, for brushing
For the filling
500g (1¼lb) fresh spinach, washed and thoroughly dried
2½ tsp fine salt
1 medium onion, peeled and very finely chopped
2 tbsp olive oil
2 tbsp sumac (from Middle Eastern shops)
a large handful pine nuts
a knob butter
5 tbsp lemon juice
1 tsp freshly ground black pepper

Put the yeast and sugar in half the warm water and leave until it bubbles.

Put the flour and salt in a large mixing bowl and make a well in the middle. Add the oil and yeast. Knead the dough for 15–20 minutes until nice and soft. Add the rest of the water bit by bit; you may not need all of it. Put the bowl in a warm spot with a cloth over it and leave for 1½–2 hours until doubled in size.

Time to prepare the filling. Put the spinach and 1 tsp of the salt in a bowl and rub them together until the spinach reduces down. Chop the spinach (we do *not* cook it). Fry the onion in the oil until transparent, then stir in the sumac. Mix the spinach with the onion. Fry the pine nuts in the butter until light golden brown and then stir into the spinach with the lemon juice and pepper.

Preheat the oven to 180°C/gas mark 4 and grease a baking tray or two. Knead the dough a little, then divide it into about thirty pieces and roll them out into 7.5cm (3in) rounds. Put about 1 tsp of the spinach filling into the middle of each circle. Using your finger, wet the edge of the circle and fold over the pastry, pinching it closed.

Put the pastries on a baking tray, brush with butter and bake for 20–30 minutes until light golden. God, these are good!

Hummus for Starters

The hummus at Abu Ahmed's was quite delicious. I can still hear my mum's warnings as my sisters and I greedily tore into our pitta breads, keen to devour the lot, it always being one of the first dishes to be served. 'You're going to fill yourselves up and there are ninety-nine more dishes to come. I promise you, you will simply explode if you eat like that!'

SERVES 4–6

2 x 400g (14oz) cans chickpeas in brine (or use dried: just soak overnight then simmer in unsalted water for an hour, or until soft)
1–3 garlic cloves, peeled and crushed
4–6 tbsp tahini
juice of 1 large, very juicy lemon, or 2 more feeble lemons
a large glug olive oil
salt

For the topping
4 tbsp pine nuts
3 large glugs olive oil
115g (4oz) leg of lamb, cut into very small cubes
1 tsp baharat spice mix (see page 120)
black pepper
chopped parsley

Empty the chickpeas and their brine into a pan and warm through. Drain, reserving the liquid. Put the chickpeas into a liquidizer with the garlic, tahini, lemon juice, olive oil and a very good pinch of salt. Blend and add a little of the reserved liquid if the mixture is too thick. I like the consistency to be a bit like thick mashed potato, but you can have it chunkier or creamier. Dip your finger in and taste. If you're still not sure, a good tip is that if the mixture has turned a creamy white, you know you've added enough lemon. Persevere: it's quite tricky to get the balance right.

When you're satisfied, start on the topping. Simply fry the pine nuts in a little of the olive oil till golden, and set aside. Then add a little more oil and, when it's nice and hot, throw in the lamb, spice and pepper and fry until it's just sealed: the pinker the better for this dish.

Spread the hummus over a large plate. Sprinkle the pine nuts and lamb around the edge and some parsley in the middle. Finish with a flourish of olive oil. Serve with plenty of hot pitta bread (see page 136).

Courgette Muttabal

This is another easy but deliciously summery dip, although I usually serve it as part of a meze. It goes beautifully alongside any plain meat or fish.

SERVES 6 AS PART OF A MEZE
450g (1lb) courgettes (if possible, the pale green ones
   from Middle Eastern shops)
olive oil
2 large garlic cloves, peeled
salt
juice of 1 or 2 lemons
4–6 tbsp tahini, loosened with a little warm water

Peel the courgettes, then cut them into thick slices. Heat a good tbsp oil and a few tbsp water and steam-fry the courgettes in a covered pan until lovely and soft.

If you have a pestle and mortar, pound the garlic with 2 tsp salt, add the courgettes and pound until smooth. My auntie always used to leave the mixture in the fridge overnight — but I don't really know why!

When ready to serve, stir in most of the lemon juice, then gradually add the tahini. Beat well and adjust the flavour with more lemon juice, salt and a good slosh of oil.

I always decorate this with criss-crossed lines of sumac (a lovely lemony spice, available from Middle Eastern shops), mostly because of its gorgeous colour but also because I'm obsessed with the flavour. Auntie Jamileh sprinkles dried mint on hers. You could also put a little heap of pomegranate seeds in the middle, or parsley. Experiment! Again, warmed pitta bread (see page 136) is my bread of choice with this.

Foul (*pronounced 'fule'*) *Medames* (*A Rich Dip for the Poor*)

In the Middle East this is known as the dish of the poor, as the ingredients are very cheap, but rest assured there's nothing cheap about the flavour. It is absolutely delicious (everyone I have ever made it for has demanded the recipe) and an added bonus is that the fava beans, garlic, parsley and olive oil make it highly nutritious.

SERVES 2–3
3 tbsp tahini
lemon juice to taste (I use a whole lemon)
a large pinch salt
2 tbsp warm water
2 large garlic cloves, peeled and chopped
400g (14oz) can cooked foul medames or fava beans
   (from Middle Eastern/Turkish shops)
For the garnish
a little chopped garlic
cayenne pepper
fresh parsley, chopped
1 hard-boiled egg per person, peeled and quartered
olive oil

Put the tahini into a small bowl and gradually mix in the lemon juice and salt until the mixture begins to go whitish. Then add enough warm water to give you a mixture the consistency of double cream. Add the chopped garlic.

Gently heat the beans in their liquid, then mash with a fork, leaving a few of the beans whole. Put into a wide serving bowl and drizzle the tahini sauce over it.

Sprinkle the chopped garlic, cayenne pepper and parsley over the top. Arrange the quartered eggs and finish off with a drizzle of olive oil. (If you like fresh chillies, why not throw some chopped ones over the top as well — Dad always does.) Serve with hot pitta bread (see page 136).

▲▽▲▽▲▽▲▽▲▽

Beautiful Beetroot Dip

When the fabulously deep purple of the beetroot is puréed with the tahini and lemon juice, this dip is transformed into an almost neon pink. Absolutely fabulous, darling! Try it with white fish, chicken or even in a cheese sandwich.

SERVES 6–8 AS PART OF A MEZE
3 large beetroot, cooked
1 tsp salt
2 garlic cloves, peeled and crushed (optional)
60ml (2 fl. oz) lemon juice
125ml (4 fl. oz) tahini
55ml (2 fl. oz) warm water

Mash the beetroot to a purée, or leave a bit more texture, whichever you prefer.

In a separate bowl mix together the salt, garlic, lemon juice, tahini and water until smooth and creamy. Add a little more water if the tahini goes sticky, and keep stirring. Now stir in the beetroot.

Serve with warm pitta bread (see page 136), or crisp Cos lettuce leaves to dip and scoop.

The Baharat Spice Trail

Believe me, this recipe makes enough for an army (so feel free to make half the amount). That said, once you've made it, you'll end up using it all the time — and given it makes such a racket to grind it all up, why not just jump in and make enough for an army!

Baharat is the Arabic word for spice, deriving from the word for pepper. It's used all over the Middle East, especially in Jordan, Syria and the Lebanon, and every country has its own particular spice mix. This is our very own special family mix and we use it with almost everything.

MAKES ... A LOT!
6 tbsp black peppercorns
3 tbsp each coriander seeds, cassia bark, cloves
  and cumin seeds
2 tsp cardamom seeds, from crushed pods
4 whole nutmegs
40g (1½oz) paprika

Grind all the spices together (you've been warned it will make a hell of a racket). This will keep for a long, long time, so long as you store it in an airtight container.

The Sawalha Barbie Girls

Dad: 'Why don't you just throw it in the oven, for God's sake?'
Mum: 'Because then it wouldn't be a bloody barbecue, would it?'

I can't remember the suggestion of a barbecue at my parents' house ever being met in any way other than the above. My dad quite simply hates them — mainly, it has to be said, because he just hasn't got the patience to wait for perfectly smoky tender meat, lovingly nurtured on an open fire. No. He's constantly piping up with alternative, speedier cooking processes. Boil it! Fry it! Fling it in the pressure cooker! Eventually we get thoroughly fed up with him and either tell him to bugger off or buy his patience with a small plate of hummus, a soothing pat on the head and a small cold glass of arak.

Bless him, after all these years he still just doesn't get it: the Sawalha girls actually *adore* the hours of preparation that go into making a perfect barbie. We relish marinating the meat, chopping the salads, tasting, chatting and arguing about what goes best with what, whilst all the while enjoying a steady stream of ice-cold glasses of wine.

There's nothing quite like the breezy smell of charcoal on a beautiful summer's day. The warm, sunny sense of expectation as we lay our huge garden table with the colourful array of bowls and plates we've gathered from our various travels is our favourite way to escape the world. Somehow, the simple act of lighting a barbecue simultaneously ignites sun-soaked memories of treasured holidays in farflung places.

Generally, though, once my father's fury and incomprehension have subsided and we girls are all on our backs, full to the gills with food and fizzy wine, you can see Dad sifting around in the coals, hunting out any glorious meaty titbits we may have forgotten!

Parsley Tahini Dip

This is such a fabulously versatile summer dip that I beg you to try it. It is the perfect partner for barbecued or grilled fish, lamb or chicken and, for all vegans, it's lovely poured over steamed vegetables or dipped into with a hunk of hot pitta bread. The vitamin-rich, vibrant green parsley, the lemon and the garlic also make it incredibly healthy. So pleasing to the eye *and* the body!

SERVES 6 AS PART OF A MEZE
1 tsp salt (though it is a case of taste, taste, taste)
1–2 garlic cloves, peeled and roughly chopped
300ml (½ pint) white tahini (the wholefood one just won't do!)
juice of 2 lemons (again, this depends on your palate)
warm water to thin
a *very* large handful fresh parsley, finely chopped

You can use a garlic press, but I love to make this in the pestle and mortar. Put the salt and garlic into the mortar and pound until it's really smooth. Pour in the tahini and mix; a whisk is best. Add the lemon juice and keep whisking. When it looks really strange and sticky, start to pour in the warm water, whisking all the while. It's ready when it looks like double cream. Stir in the lusciously green parsley.

Tahini Sauce

A delicious sauce that can also be served with fish, any grilled meat or, if thinned down a little more, as a salad dressing.

SERVES 4–6 AS PART OF A MEZE
4 tbsp tahini
3 tbsp lemon juice
salt
2–6 tbsp warm water

Put the tahini, lemon juice and salt in a small bowl, then gradually add the water whilst whisking. You may need to add more water if it's sticky. This should end up the consistency of double cream.

Tabbouleh

I love to sit with my sisters, aunties, cousins or friends and make this.
I call it 'the gossip dish'. It takes quite a long time to chop all the
ingredients as small as they need to be, so, as far as I'm concerned,
it's a perfect opportunity for mindless but soothing tittle-tattle
and plenty of vino!

SERVES 4–6 AS PART OF A MEZE
200g (7oz) burghul wheat
salt
½ cucumber, seeded and very finely chopped
2 medium tomatoes, skinned, seeded and cut into tiny cubes
3 tbsp spring onions (as fresh as can be), finely chopped
3 tbsp very finely chopped fresh mint
200g (7oz) very finely chopped fresh parsley (it will have to be
   completely dry to be able to chop it as finely as you need to)
4 tbsp lemon juice (to taste)
4–6 tbsp olive oil (to taste)
1 Cos lettuce

Put the burghul wheat into a bowl with a couple of tsp salt and cover with hot
water. Leave to soak for 30 minutes. Salt the cucumber and leave it to drain
in a colander for 30 minutes.

You will need to stand a tea-towel-lined colander in the sink. Drain the
soaked burghul and put it into the colander. To get every last bit of it dry,
take each corner of the tea-towel and twist and squeeze the water out.

Put the burghul into a mixing bowl and stir in all the other ingredients,
including the cucumber, tasting and adjusting all the way.

This salad looks simply spectacular in a glass bowl, especially if you line
it with Cos lettuce leaves, all standing to attention, and pile the salad up
in the middle. It will glisten and twinkle magically!

Shish Taouk — It's Thyme for Kebabs

This is a very popular dish with my family. The purists amongst them would not add fresh thyme, but being the rebel that I am, I put in lots! If you have a friendly butcher, get him to bone some chicken thighs for you. If you're anything like me, you'll always end up making an absolute mess if you try to do it yourself. The thigh meat is really tasty, but this is traditionally made with breast, so I do a mixture of both. Mark won't touch anything but the breast anyway … I found this out when we first met.

SERVES 8

4 boneless, skinned chicken breasts, diced into
   2.5cm (1in) cubes
6 boned chicken thighs, cubed as above

For the marinade

6–8 plump garlic cloves, peeled and pounded
   until creamy
4 juicy lemons
a handful fresh thyme
1 tsp cayenne pepper
a few glugs olive oil
lots of crunchy salt

Have your barbecue coals ready, and soak your wooden skewers, if using them.

Put the chicken breasts and thigh meat in two separate bowls and share out the marinade ingredients between them, giving it all a good old mix. The longer you leave this marinating, the more tender and delicious it will be. I have to admit, though, that I hardly ever have time to leave it for more than about 15 minutes, and it's *still* good. But do leave time to soak the skewers if you're using wooden ones, to prevent them catching fire.

Whenever you're ready, thread the chicken breast and thigh meat on to separate skewers and put them on to your hot, white coals. Nurse them by turning and basting them until cooked through and golden, with lovely little charred bits round the edges. This will take very little time: about 8 minutes. If you haven't got time to mess about with a barbecue, they can be grilled and will take about the same amount of time.

I like to wrap my chicken in hot flatbread with a sprinkle of tabbouleh and a drizzle of tahini sauce (see pages 124 and 122).

Popping Carrot Salad

This is one of my all-time favourite salads, and it has the added and rather unusual (for a salad) bonus of actually improving in flavour if made an hour or so before you eat it; it even tastes good the next day. Please don't stick rigidly to the amounts. I like my carrot salad to be really lemony and salty, which my mum doesn't like at all — in fact, she puts only two or three big squeezes of lemon in hers. When I have some of this left over, I make a sandwich with it, adding a big spoonful of hummus or cheese — mmm, delicious.

SERVES 10–12 AS PART OF A MEZE
1kg (2¼lb) organic carrots (they really must taste
    preservative-free)
salt
juice of 2 juicy lemons
8 tbsp vegetable oil
2 tbsp mustard seeds (optional)
4 tbsp nigella seeds (black onion seeds; from Indian shops)

Peel and finely grate the carrots and put them into a salad bowl. Salt well and stir in the lemon juice.

Heat the oil in a frying pan and fry the mustard seeds and nigella seeds for a few seconds until they begin to pop and the nigella seeds start to release their aroma. Tip immediately over the salad and mix them in.

My Arabic Salad

I serve this lovely fresh salad with meat, fish, chicken, baked potatoes and falafel. But, sometimes, without telling anyone, I just make a huge bowl of it and eat the lot entirely on its own!

SERVES 4
1 red onion, peeled and very thinly sliced
juice of 1 lemon
3 tomatoes, cubed
2 small Middle Eastern cucumbers, cubed
1 small Cos lettuce, chopped
1 small green pepper, seeded and thinly sliced
1 tbsp chopped fresh parsley
1 pitta bread, cut into squares and fried in olive oil
For the dressing
3 tbsp olive oil
3 tbsp lemon juice
1 garlic clove, peeled and crushed
1 tsp sumac (from Middle Eastern shops)
1 tbsp chopped fresh mint
salt

First macerate the red onion in the lemon juice for 10 minutes.

For the dressing, put the oil, lemon juice and garlic in a small bowl, stir well, then add the remaining ingredients.

Put all the vegetables into a bowl and, just before you serve, add the fried pitta bread and pour the dressing over it.

Desperately Seeking Shawarma

It's midnight and my family and I are hurtling along the streets of downtown Amman in my uncle's mustard-coloured, bashed-up old Volvo. It's like a scene from a movie: a crazed car chase in which no one is being chased, yet everyone's chasing; the combined cacophony of car horns all blending into one enormous, insane BEEEEP!

Adding to the mayhem, my father and uncle gabble on incessantly, desperate to make up for months of lost sibling time. My sisters and I hang out of the car windows, relishing the warm air brushing our cheeks and the sweet, heady smell of jasmine strangely mixed with car fumes. Unbelievably, just 5 hours ago we were queuing in a miserably cold Heathrow airport, and now we're part of the hurtling chaos of my father's homeland.

We've been in the country for no more than half an hour, but we're already on our way to our favourite 'dining establishment' — a place my sisters and I have been dreaming about ever since our plane tickets ceremoniously thumped on to our doormat a few weeks ago.

My uncle weaves his way through myriad winding streets, finally screeching to a halt and abandoning the car in the middle of the road. We all pile out eagerly, dashing down a busy alleyway teeming with life: left and right, old men sipping Arabic coffee, street-sellers peddling their wares, indomitable women shouting at small boys; all brought together as childhood memory by the thick aroma of the hubbly-bubblies assaulting our senses; always in the distance, just out of reach, the smell of tahini teasing us ever onwards like the original Bisto Kids.

Finally, the alleyway widens and we arrive at the tiniest of openings, brimming with people and noise. To the untrained eye, it appears to be a throng of people all madly speaking, gesticulating, pushing and shoving. At the centre hangs a flickering fluorescent light, accompanied by a blaring television screen transmitting no picture, just the berating racket of an Egyptian newsreader's voice.

This place serves the best shawarma anywhere on the planet, and everyone in Amman knows it. No longer repressed by the British obsession for forming orderly queues, my family and I tentatively join in, giving our fellow diners a little shove here, a nudge or two there, a jab of the elbow for good measure. Before you know it, we're at the counter, drooling at the sight and smell of my favourite dish of all time: something that would definitely be my last supper (alongside roast chicken). I have a lot of last-supper favourites, which must mean on some level I have a deathwish. No, seriously, shawarma is my homecoming dream: slivers of lamb exquisitely marinated in an abundance of exotic spices, lemon and fresh herbs, then barbecued on a rotating spike until cooked to melting perfection.

My uncle puts in our order, hands over a few tarnished old coins and the shop-owner swirls into action, immediately unsheathing the longest, sharpest knife imaginable. I hold my breath, and with what appears to be just four flashes of his blade, he shaves off slice after slice of the fragrant sticky lamb, then lays them on the thinnest Arabic bread (freshly baked that morning). Home-made pickles and creamy tahini sauce are added before he wraps everything in greaseproof paper to make a 'perfect-to-hold-in-your-hand' roll.

As this truly magical gift is given to us, we girls devour them within seconds, paying no heed to the thin lines of tahini sauce dripping down our chins as newly impatient customers try to jostle us out of their way.

This is *the* shawarma experience! In fact, my tip for this recipe is that when you make them at home, invite as many friends and family over as possible. Once they've arrived, all stand in the smallest part of the kitchen and proceed to devour them whilst forcibly using your elbows to push everyone around you out of the way. Close your eyes, sniff and I promise you — you'll immediately be transported to downtown Amman!

Shawarma

It's taken me years to get this recipe just right, and along the way many of my relatives have told me not to bother trying as it's 'impossible to get the right taste' … So here I go blowing my own trumpet again, but I think this recipe gets pretty damn close!

SERVES 4–6
450g (1lb) leg of lamb meat, cut into really thin strips
2 tbsp cider vinegar
juice of 1 juicy lemon
1 tsp finely grated lemon zest
1 tsp each ground cinnamon and ground allspice
1 tsp each salt and black pepper
½ tsp ground cardamom
3 pieces mastic (grind this really fine between 2 spoons
   with a little sugar)
1 small onion, peeled and grated
1 small tomato, grated
3 glugs olive oil
5 tbsp finely chopped fresh parsley
To serve
pitta bread (see page 136), or wraps
tahini sauce (see page 122)
my Arabic salad (see page 130), omitting the pitta bread

Put all the shawarma ingredients in a bowl and leave in the fridge for 24 hours. Give it a good stir every now and then.

Take it out of the fridge an hour before you need it and put it in a sieve or on a rack to drain.

Now, naturally, this is divine cooked on the barbie, but remember it will only take a minute or so on each side to cook. If a barbecue is not on the agenda, a really hot grill will do.

Have warmed pitta bread ready and waiting and simply nestle the lamb into it, add the salad and drizzle the tahini sauce all over. Now you have permission to get messy!

Alternatively, lay a warmed tortilla on top of a piece of greaseproof paper (take the time to do this, as it makes a big difference), put the lamb, salad and tahini sauce on top of it, then roll it into a hold-in-your-hand tight roll.

Perfect Pittas

'On my family's bread, I swear I am telling the truth' — Palestinian saying

Don't get me wrong: nine times out of ten I buy my pitta bread and it's fine, but of course it's nowhere near as good as home-made.

MAKES 8–10

300 ml (½ pint) warm water (not too warm or you will kill
   the yeast)
10g (¼oz) dried yeast
1 tsp caster sugar
450g (1lb) strong white bread flour, plus extra for dusting
1 tsp fine salt
sunflower oil

Put the water, yeast and sugar into a bowl. Stir and leave in a warm place for about 10 minutes until magically it begins to froth. (It doesn't matter how many times I see this happen, I'm always thrilled.)

Now sift the flour and salt into a bowl, make a well in the middle and add the yeast mixture. Mix together, adding a good glug of oil and a little more water, bit by bit, if needed (we're after a firm, soft dough).

Put the dough on to a floured surface and knead until it's like elastic. I'm afraid this takes a good 10–15 minutes and my woefully under-exercised body feels the pain! If you're lucky enough to have a mixer with a dough hook, bung it in there. Once kneaded to perfection, cover with a clean, damp tea-towel and leave in a nice warm spot for 2 hours (or until it's done its magic again and doubled in size).

Punch it down and knead lightly. Divide into eight or ten equal pieces about the size of golf balls. Put them on a floured tray, cover with a floured tea-towel and leave for another 20 minutes before rolling them out. Shake a little flour over them, cover and leave for yet another 30 minutes, then roll them out and sprinkle them very lightly with water (so they don't colour).

Preheat the oven to its highest temperature, then bake the pittas until they're beautifully puffed up (about 7–10 minutes) but have a peep after 6 minutes (not before!).

Comfort Food

Hey Diddle Dee Dee,
An Actor's Life For Me!

The first my parents knew of my ambitions to be a performer was when, at the ripe old age of twelve, I stormed into their bedroom at the crack of dawn and announced that, unless they allowed me to audition for the famous Italia Conti stage school, I'd throw myself out of the window there and then. Poor things, they were utterly unprepared for this outburst as, up until the day before, my all-consuming ambition as far as they were concerned had been to be a nurse!

Where had this turnaround come from? Why had I turned my back on an important and caring profession that changes and transforms lives in order to seek a career in which paranoia, rejection and the constant hope of applause were the main factors? Well, my parents were oblivious to the fact that just a few weeks before, their incredibly enthusiastic reaction to my first stab at acting and singing in a school play had been a totally life-changing experience. I had found my calling, *darrrling*! My path was now inextricably mapped out. Nothing could (or would) stand in my way!

Presented with such an ultimatum they could do little but allow me to audition (not thinking for a moment that I'd actually get in). Bless them. What a horrible shock when I won a much-coveted place. As my mother so aptly put it to my dad (who was by now rocking back and forth with the horror of his daughter following in his footsteps), 'You do realize we're going to have to let the little madam go now, don't you?' (I know of this exchange because I was eavesdropping from my usual vantage point at the corner banister.) My father replied, 'What were you thinking, Betty? Why did you let her audition?', thus transferring *all* responsibility for my career path to my mother.

Within a few months I was happily ensconced in the rarefied world of the Italia Conti stage school. Think *Fame* the movie (the original film, of course) but set it in Stockwell rather than New York and *wham* — to quote the song, I was going to live for ever!

Just seventy kids attended, plucked from the length and breadth of the country, and every single one of them wanted to be there more than anything (or anyone) else in the world. So, as you can imagine, the atmosphere was totally exhilarating as well as terrifyingly competitive. A unique school experience. In one fell swoop I went from Latin and algebra and a future of nurses' uniforms to show tunes and drama. I loved every minute!

I bet you're thinking, how is she going to get food into this story? Trust me, I'm getting there. Because everyone at the school was constantly watching their weight (with the sole exception of me, it has to be said), all our food was cooked on the premises to make sure it was healthy and not too calorific. But, somewhere along the line, one of the canteen ladies took pity on us and this philosophy fell to pieces, as there were always sausage rolls and cheese chunks on sale. Could there be anything more fattening? Those of us who weren't planning careers as dancers would peel open a piping-hot sausage roll and wedge in a chunk of Cheddar cheese, causing it to go perfectly melty. I'm drooling at the memory … It is the top comfort food ever, and so utterly decadent in its disregard for the human body that you have to try it at least once.

Blistering Hot Sausage Roll and Cheddar Cheese

Don't be tempted, as I once was, to cook the cheese in with the sausage roll. It is so, *so* wrong. Part of the heavenliness of this indulgence is the contrast between the piping-hot sausagemeat, the melty outside of the cheese and the cold last bite through to the centre.

(My sister Julia called just as I was writing this. When I told her what I was writing about she said I have to tell you that she used to dip hers in salad cream. I ask you! It's a good job she's a vegan now ...)

SERVES 4–6
225g (8oz) sausagemeat
1 onion, peeled and finely chopped
1 tsp each finely chopped fresh sage and parsley
salt and plenty of black pepper
1 packet ready-rolled puff pastry
a little plain flour, if necessary
1 egg yolk, whisked with a little milk
To serve
about 115g (4oz) Cheddar

Preheat the oven to 200°C/gas mark 6 and grease a baking tray.

Mix together the sausagemeat, onion and herbs, and season well. Pop back in the fridge until ready to use.

Now lay out the pastry on your work surface and cut it lengthways into two pieces. Take out the sausagemeat and divide it into two pieces. Roll the pieces out into two long sausages; if it feels a bit soggy, add a little flour. Now lay them on the pastry, leaving them about 2.5cm (1in) from the edge. With a pastry brush (if you have one, otherwise do what I do and use your fingers), brush the edge of the pastry with some of the egg wash and fold the pastry over the meat, rolling it as you do. Cut the two long rolls into smaller rolls.

Now it's time to put them on a greased baking tray, making sure that the sealed side is on the base. Brush with more of the egg mixture and pop them into the oven for about 20–25 minutes. They should be a nice golden brown before you take them out.

Whilst they're still piping hot, carefully open up the rolls, put a thick wedge of Cheddar in and close up the pastry. Eat as fast as you can.

Egg and Twigs!

For the past twenty years or so, there's been an ongoing row between myself, my sister Julia and our dear friend Janine over who exactly was the genius matchmaker who decided to bring these two lovebird ingredients together: soft, creamy boiled eggs and tangy Twiglets to dip. What a pairing!

I once did a dating show called *Perfect Partners* and never has there been a more accurate description of this most divine of couplings. Delectable, drippy egg yolk, all ruffled and disturbed by a crispy Marmitey Twiglet. What can I say? Perfect Partners! So who was the clever matchmaker? What cupid of culinary love fired that first Twiglet arrow into that gloopy yellow heart of an egg?

Well! I'm going to put an end to all the wrangling and disputes once and for all. It was ME! ALL ME! So, shove that in yer egg yolk, Julia and Janine!

I promise you, try this combination on your kids and they'll adore it. That's why mine have nicknamed this highly sophisticated dish 'Egg and Twigs'!

SERVES 1
2 large organic eggs
salt
2 handfuls Twiglets

Put the eggs in a pan of cold water with a large pinch of salt. (I do this with my boiled eggs simply because my mum always does. Apparently it stops the egg running out if it's cracked, though I'm not really sure about this!) Bring to the boil and simmer for 3 minutes.

Now dip with the twigs! (I have been known to dip the twigs in butter first!)

Creamy Pea and Bacon Pasta

Although I've instructed you in this recipe to add 4 tablespoons of mascarpone cheese to your pasta, it is actually rather naughty of me to do so, because I always end up adding a lot more than that. I suppose I just didn't want to reveal to you the extent of my greed!

SERVES 4–6
400g (14oz) pasta
salt and black pepper
175g (6oz) frozen or fresh podded peas
2 tbsp olive oil
150g (5½oz) smoked lardons or streaky bacon
1 small onion, peeled and finely chopped
1 fat garlic clove, peeled and finely chopped
2 small dried chillies, crumbled
4 tbsp cream cheese (mascarpone is yum here,
    but use whatever you have)
as much freshly grated Parmesan as you like
a big handful fresh basil leaves, torn

Put plenty of salted water into the biggest saucepan you have and bring to the boil. Add the pasta and cook until al dente. Throw in the peas for the last few minutes of cooking. Drain.

While all this is going on, heat the olive oil in a heavy frying pan, throw in the bacon and cook until it becomes just crisp. Remove with a slotted spoon. Now put in the onion, garlic and chillies, and fry until soft. Put the bacon back in and cook altogether for a minute or so.

Add the drained pasta and peas. Stir in the cheeses, lots of freshly ground black pepper and the basil. Once, when I made this, I had some leftover roasted almonds from a dinner party my mum had had the night before, so, in my greedy fashion, I sprinkled them on top of the pasta; surprisingly, it was a really good mixture.

Guilty Secrets

Fried chicken is a real favourite amongst the kids in the family, but, as usual with my lot, they all have their likes and dislikes, which is why I always end up having to cook endless different varieties: one without garlic, another without chilli, one with gluten-free flour and another (really, really annoyingly) without salt! I know what you're thinking: 'She must be mad spoiling them like that!' And I'd have to say, 'Yes, you're right, I *am* mad. They *are* spoilt! So, shoot me!'

Because I don't want to bore you with every permutation of fried chicken ever to have emerged from my kitchen, I'm only going to share with you the recipe I use for me and possibly the biggest kid in the family, my dad — a recipe, incidentally, that I pull out on the quiet whenever my mum isn't anywhere to be seen; usually when she's on one of her monthly stocking-up missions to France. On these occasions my father usually wanders around in our gardens like a lost goat in the middle of the desert, picking at scraps of cereal, rancid nuts and half-eaten apples left in the larder. Also, whenever he is lost and hungry he generally (for some bizarre reason) goes on a massive building binge. I swear that most of the many extensions he has built on his house, and some of the extra rooms he has added to ours, were a consequence of a raging appetite. My husband Mark will often say something like, 'I think your dad might be hungry. He's just started to build another outhouse in the garden.'

Making matters worse, whenever my mother goes AWOL leaving Dad home alone, my nephew Zak (who now lives with them) usually slips through the front door at some point, hiding a famously branded bucket of chicken pieces, the smell of which always leaves my dad feeling very sorry for himself, and even hungrier ...

That is, until *I* walk in, my arms filled with bags of shopping. 'Ahhh, Nadia. How wonderful to see you, darling,' he invariably says, before tentatively fishing: 'Have you eaten?'

Of course, he knows very well I haven't eaten: he also knows very well that I've come over to spoil him with his absolute favourite, kickin' fried chicken. And boy, does this have a kick!

KFC *(Kickin' Fried Chicken)*

This is an absolutely foolproof recipe, because the chicken is already cooked through. Just make sure your oil is nice and hot and that you have brought it up to heat gradually, and then you will get a lovely golden-brown crust.

SERVES 4
8 chicken pieces
1.2 litres (2 pints) full-fat milk
salt
1 bouquet garni
175g (6oz) plain flour
2 tbsp cayenne pepper
3 tsp freshly ground black pepper
2 tsp ground each ground cumin and ground coriander
1 tsp each ground turmeric and garam masala
1 tsp dried chilli or chilli powder
2 eggs, beaten
groundnut oil for deep-frying

Put the chicken pieces in a bowl and pour on the milk so they're completely immersed. If you have time, cover and put in the fridge overnight, as this makes the meat lovely and soft.

Pour the chicken and milk into a pan, then add some salt and the bouquet garni. Cover, bring to a bubble and let it simmer for about 15–20 minutes, until the chicken is cooked through. Take the chicken pieces out of the milk and let them cool off a little bit.

Now get two bowls: in one put the flour and all the spices, and in the other the beaten eggs. Roll the chicken in the flour, then in the egg and then back in the flour. It's mucky but fun!

Now bring the oil up to heat: you'll know it's ready when a tiny piece of bread bubbles fiercely and turns brown in under a minute. Gently lower the chicken pieces in. As they're already cooked through, you need only cook them long enough to turn them a perfect golden brown — just a few minutes. Dad and I adore my celeriac coleslaw (see opposite) with this: it makes us feel *très, très* posh.

Celeriac Coleslaw

This is rather special coleslaw, which needs only a little more effort to make than 'coleslaw-coleslaw', but is definitely worth the extra faff.

SERVES 4
1 small celeriac, peeled and grated
2 tbsp sunflower oil
1 tbsp white wine vinegar
½ tsp fine salt
½ the weight of carrots to celeriac
a handful rocket leaves
fresh chives, chopped
For the dressing
6 tbsp home-made mayonnaise (see page 235)
½ tsp French mustard
½ small garlic clove, peeled and finely chopped

Mix the celeriac, oil, vinegar and salt in a bowl and leave to marinate overnight.

Drain the celeriac and put it into a serving bowl. Peel and grate the carrots and mix into the celeriac with the rocket and chives. Mix together the mayonnaise, mustard and garlic, pour over the vegetables and give it all a really good stir.

Posh Tomato Soup

Right. I have a guilty secret. I just *love* Heinz tomato soup. There you go — at last, I've said it. In my own cookbook. I have another confession: I like it with lots and lots of plastic white bread slathered with thick layers of salty butter. I feel like a free woman now!

I think it's fair to say that there are certain times in a girl's life when only this smooth, tomatoey tonic will do: like when you've been dumped, or when you have the hangover from hell, or maybe when you're half dead from yet another sleepless night with one of your little darlings. These are all occasions when minimum effort and maximum speed are needed to produce a comforting 'meal' that temporarily heals the soul.

With Heinz doing their bit for the downtimes in life, my recipe for tomato soup is for the uptimes! Those days when you're fit as a fiddle, irritatingly buoyant, feel like doing the spring cleaning and are happy to let your lunch happily pop and bubble away on the stove for a good hour or so. This takes a while to cook, but I promise it gives a lovingly long hug in return.

SERVES 6
olive oil
1 medium onion, peeled and chopped
3 celery sticks, chopped
2 carrots, peeled and chopped
1 garlic clove, peeled and chopped
1kg (2¼lb) fresh tomatoes, chopped
a pinch caster sugar
a large pinch dried oregano
salt and black pepper
1.5 litres (2¾ pints) stock (chicken or vegetable concentrate)
2 tbsp mascarpone cheese
fresh basil leaves, torn

Put 2–3 glugs olive oil into a heavy pan and gently fry the chopped onion, celery and carrot until soft. Then throw in the garlic and cook for a minute. Now add the luscious red tomatoes, stir in the sugar and oregano, and season with salt and pepper. Bring to the boil, then add the stock. Turn the heat down, cover and simmer for 30 minutes.

When it's all beautifully soft, whizz in the blender. Whisk in the mascarpone and serve sprinkled with torn fresh basil leaves.

Mackerel Pâté for Grown-ups

I always felt terribly sophisticated when I made this, and suitably rebellious. In my teens I would simply use mackerel bought from the supermarket, but my goodness, now that I've discovered the joys of my fishmonger and his beautifully smoked mackerel (soft, smoky and tender), I can never go back!

SERVES 4–6

300g (10½oz) your favourite cream cheese
1 smoked mackerel, flaked (from the fishmonger if possible;
    you will need 2 if from the supermarket)
2–3 tbsp horseradish cream
finely grated zest and juice of ½ lemon
a couple tbsp chopped fresh parsley
freshly ground black pepper

Deliciously easy! Simply put everything into a bowl and mix. I like it quite chunky and lumpy, but it can be made as smooth as butter if you prefer.

It's really lovely spread on granary toast with sliced cucumber and watercress, but sometimes I just eat it with a spoon …

Me all grown up at eighteen years old.

Honestly, what a show-off!

The Devil's Work

I call this dish 'The Devil's Work' because it is so utterly fattening and so utterly irresistible!

SERVES 2 GREEDY OR 4 NORMAL PEOPLE
8 slices white bread
about 175–200g (6–7oz) butter
4 tbsp jam (I like raspberry with this)
For the batter
55g (2oz) plain flour
1 large egg, whisked
100ml (3½fl. oz) full-fat milk, mixed with 40ml (1½fl. oz) water
2 tsp vanilla extract

For the batter, sift the flour into a bowl and make a well in the centre. Add the egg, then slowly pour in the milk-and-water mixture, whisking the whole time. Now stir in the vanilla extract and inhale its heady scent — a real cook's pleasure!

Spread the bread with butter on one side (leaving some for the frying). Cut the crusts off, then spread on lots of lovely jam and make into sandwiches. Cut them into squares, stars, hearts, whatever you fancy.

Dip the sandwich shapes into the batter, then fry in the remaining butter until golden brown. Cor blimey, what a treat!

The hangovers were unbelievable...

Cheap and Cheerful
Chomping

Cheap and Cheerful Chomping

In my early teens, rather unsurprisingly, I rebelled. Not in the conventional ways of slamming doors, staying out late and treating the house like a hotel (though these weren't a million miles away!). No, the rebellion *I* began was more against my culinary past.

As you'll have gathered, not only were my father's family evangelical about food, but also the theatre and razzamatazz involved with eating it was often so spectacularly exhausting that just good ole-fashioned cheese on toast was often a much-desired alternative.

As for Mum's cuisine, well, although I adored it, let's face it, as a teen — it *was* after all my *mother's* food. However good it may have been, the teenage shame of one's parents also, sadly, spreads to their cooking.

At sixteen the headline thought was how best to achieve a maximum culinary punch with an absolute minimum of effort. But also these swift and tasty recipes *had* to be my *own* creations, clear of family opinion, away from their prying eyes, definitely away from their voracious appetites, and most certainly away from their now deeply embarrassing parties!

This was when I started truly to create dishes that were entirely mine. I suppose in a way it was time for me to navigate a course between my parents' two cuisines and so I found myself exploring my own British culinary roots — still relatively uncharted waters in our household.

I wanted to create the kind of food with which I could impress my mates. Easy on the pocket. Easy on the palate. Easy to make, and easy on the eye. With all those strange teenage hormones coursing through my veins, all I wanted (if totally honest) was to create ... GRUB!

I was desperate for ingredients like sausages, baked beans, that now-British classic spaghetti (!), stock cubes (this last being a direct reaction to my mother's stock, which was always home-made and lovely, but would boil for hours on end, invading every corner of the house).

The greatest thing about the dishes I magicked up as a teenage kitchen rebel is that I still use all these recipes today.

Resting Actresses

An actor's life is not always an enviable one. The beginning of any actress's career is essentially spent in a limited number of unpleasant emotional states. Very often you're paranoid ('Nobody likes me, everyone thinks I'm rubbish'), idle (because every casting director thinks you're 'not right for the job'), arrogant ('When I'm spotted I'm going to be the next Judi Dench. They don't know what they're missing!') and hungry ... very, very hungry (basically, no acting jobs equals no money equals no swanky meals). All these accurately describe me at twenty-one and Julia at seventeen.

We were actually working at the Piccadilly Theatre at the time, but we were nowhere near the stage. Instead, we were front of house tearing tickets and directing people to the loo! But we still loved every second of it, even though the experience fell far short of our dreams.

To make up for this frustration we worked hard and played even harder. After a night of steering yet more tourists towards the gents', the ladies', the stalls bar and the circle bar, we would invariably end up in the pub with a group of mates, before piling back to my flat, which was attached to the side of my parents' house.

The exact relevance of my flat's location is to do with the fact that there was a connecting door into my mum's kitchen — a door almost as exciting as the elusive 'stage door'; and it was through this door that, at some point, Julia and I would sneak to source some much-needed ingredients. When all was silent and Mum and Dad were clearly in bed, drunkenly sniggering and shushing each other we would nervously push the door open and tip-toe in to randomly grab at ingredients in the dark.

And so it was on one of these nights of thieving and grabbing that the list of ingredients overleaf emerged from our bag of culinary booty, before somehow (God only knows how, given how inebriated we all were) they were magically transformed by yours truly into a most delicious macaroni cheese.

Julia and I still reminisce about those nights and this dish, and sometimes, for old times' sake, when visiting Mum and Dad we will both creep and crawl into their kitchen in pursuit of the same tasty treasures.

'Alf-inched Macaroni Cheese

Here it is. I have to say I don't know whether it was the cheese or the pasta, or perhaps both, but whenever we ate this we rarely had a hangover the next day ...

SERVES 4
400g (14oz) macaroni (or, if resorting to theft,
    any pasta shape you can get your hands on)
salt and black pepper
1 medium onion, peeled and chopped
vegetable oil
100–200g (3½–7oz) bacon lardons or chopped smoked bacon
85g (3oz) butter
85g (3oz) plain flour
850ml (1½ pints) full-fat milk
175g (6oz) mature Cheddar, grated, plus extra for the topping
8 large sun-dried tomatoes (or however many you fancy),
    chopped
4 tbsp chopped fresh parsley
a couple of fresh tomatoes, sliced

Cook the pasta in boiling salted water according to packet instructions and drain.

Meanwhile fry the onions in a little oil until they begin to soften, then add the bacon, fry until brown and set aside.

Melt the butter in a non-stick saucepan, add the flour and stir together for a few minutes over a low heat. Keep stirring or it will stick — even to your non-stick pan!

Slowly add the milk, stirring the whole time. It will go a bit sticky and look as if it's going wrong, but stir briskly and all will be fine. Continue until all the milk has been used.

Now lower the heat and simmer for 10 minutes, stirring pretty much the whole time (it's actually quite soothing). Next add the cheese and stir until melted. Stir in the onion, bacon, sun-dried tomatoes and parsley. Do not boil, as this spoils the consistency.

Mix with the cooked, drained pasta and put into an ovenproof dish. Sprinkle the dish with extra grated cheese and lay sliced tomatoes around the edge. Grill until the cheese bubbles. I like it best when the cheese is ever so slightly burnt.

Cooking for the Cast

When I started out as an actress I spent a good couple of years touring around the country in clapped-out old mini-vans performing in *some* very good and many (it has to be said) very bad productions. Throughout this period, being 'on the road' amounted to staying in smelly old B&Bs, sharing damp bedrooms decorated with hideously peeling wallpaper with my co-actors, and suffering sudden (and sometimes prolonged) bouts of homesickness. Despite this, it was one of the most exciting times of my life. I was on the road towards realizing my acting dreams and ambitions. I was fearless. I was indestructible. And I was — well, I was hungry!

If I felt the accommodation and transportation were bad, the food was even worse. Generally, the order of the day was microwaved breakfasts, vile petrol-station sandwiches, flabby cardboard pizzas and spot-inducing, grey, greasy chips. In fact, I remember the occasional Ginsters ham and mushroom pie seeming like *haute cuisine* compared to the standard fare on offer.

Most of the time the cast and crew were absolutely desperate for any home-cooked food whatsoever, even if it was just a slice of toast and a decent cuppa. We would spend hours in transit, dreaming about and lusting after our favourite home-cooked meals. Of course I was always the most verbose on the subject, seducing them all with tales of the delicious things I was going to cook for everyone the first opportunity I got.

You see, every so often, as our theatrical troupe rolled into some regional town like Shakespeare's rabble-rousing merry players, we'd wander into a basement flat, which would be 'home' for the next fortnight, to witness one enormous living-room-cum-bedroom and a 'kitchen'. This would have a sink, an old gas hob and a small cupboard with no door. But, with the pulling up of a most theatrically mildewed curtain, a liberal sprinkling of some candlelight and several bottles of retsina, the stage would (quite quickly) be set for my culinary performance!

As I set about creating a mini-home from home, I would be in my absolute element, showing off my culinary talents to my surrogate family. Like a first night that ends with a standing ovation (not that there were ever many of them), I gloried in my co-thespians' gasps of delight as I swept in with anything from a perfectly risen toad-in-the-hole (accompanied by bowls of steaming mash and sticky onion gravy) to a truly show-offy spread in the form of that ultimate of culinary challenges — a full-on Arabic meze dinner for eight.

What was always fabulous to witness was the way in which, when they'd finished the main course, my co-actors never expected a culinary encore. How wrong could they have been? Had they forgotten — with me in the kitchen — the entire culinary show was *all* about the encore!

Dessert would be anything from piles of impressive vanilla-cream meringues (if only they'd known how easy they were) to a sweet tooth's dream of coconut treacle tarts, or maybe sometimes huge bowls of wobbly sherry trifle topped with chopped pistachio nuts.

As with most performances, the very best part of these often dimly lit, slightly damp evenings was the utterly addictive hit of watching my extremely stuffed audience slip into a well-deserved after-theatre food coma. Then and now, inducing a contented state of culinary concussion in my guests is truly one of life's greatest pleasures!

Sometimes, when my acting chums and I started to appear in shows that I now affectionately refer to as my cringe-fringe era, we'd all get together in a pub somewhere around Waterloo (if only to pretend to those who overheard our thespian ways that we were in the latest at the Old Vic) and, after ordering a round of drinks, we'd all have a whip round for dinner. As was normally the case, the piles of 10-pence pieces on the table revealed that (a) we weren't working at the Old Vic, and (b) I'd have to feed a lot of hungry actors on very limited finances. Thus the whip-round shepherd's pie was born.

The Whip-round Shepherd's Pie

I have to admit I always had to fight the urge to add some Arabic spices to this. But I'm glad I did. The subtle flavours of the lamb and rosemary are absolutely delicious with the creamy mash and don't need any further embellishment.

SERVES 4–6
675g (1½lb) minced lamb
vegetable oil
3 onions, peeled and sliced
2 celery sticks, chopped
2 carrots, peeled and diced
1–2 garlic cloves, peeled and crushed
1 dsp plain flour
a big splash Worcestershire sauce
2 tsp fresh rosemary, chopped
200ml (7 fl. oz) brown stock, mixed with 1 tbsp tomato purée
salt and black pepper
900g (2lb) Maris Piper potatoes, peeled and cut into small pieces
55g (2oz) butter
55–125ml (2–4 fl. oz) milk or single cream
salt and black pepper

Heat a heavy-based pan and fry the mince in batches in a little oil. Don't move it about too much, as the meat flavour intensifies if you let it brown. Now remove it with a slotted spoon and put it in a colander over a plate.

Throw the onion, celery, carrot and garlic (if using) into the same pan, adding a little more oil if you feel you need it. Let them cook slowly until they soften. Add the flour and let it cook for a minute or so (otherwise you'll taste it). Now everything else can go in: the drained lamb, the Worcestershire sauce, the rosemary and the stock. Season well and let it all bubble away on a very low heat for about 15 minutes, partially covered.

Meanwhile, make the mash (God, I love mash!). Boil the potatoes in salted water until perfectly tender (be patient—you don't want lumpy mash). Drain, put them back in the pan and mash with the butter, milk or cream, and season to taste.

OK, time to put the pie together! First turn on the grill. Spoon the lamb and veg into an ovenproof dish, then pile the smooth buttery mash on top. If I am having a 'sod-the-hips-day', I dot lots of extra butter over the potatoes before putting under the grill and cooking until beautifully golden brown.

I don't know about you, but for me it has to be peas with shepherd's pie.

A Teen's Toad-in-the-hole

Now be warned: if you're after a well-risen, puffy pudding, this is not the recipe for you. I love a dense texture and eggy flavour to my batter. You've been warned – but it's delicious, so why not give it a go?

SERVES 4
3–4 tbsp vegetable oil (but if you have dripping, yum, use it!)
8 finest pork sausages
For the batter
175g (6oz) plain flour
salt and black pepper
2 large free-range eggs, plus 1 egg white
300ml (½ pint) milk, mixed with 150ml (5 fl. oz) cold water
3 tbsp dripping or lard

You can make the batter the day before if you like, but if not, try to leave it to rest for at least 20 minutes. If you really haven't got time for this, you can get away with using it straight away.

Sift the flour and salt into a bowl, add some pepper, then add the eggs. Whisk together whilst slowly adding the milk (you might not need all of it), beating out any little lumps of flour as you go. The consistency should be about that of double cream, but no thinner – the batter should coat the back of a spoon. Leave to rest for 20 minutes or longer.

Preheat the oven to 220°C/gas mark 7.

I usually put the fat into the tin and brown the sausages on the top of the stove, then put the tin into the oven until the fat is really hot – smoking hot is best. Then it's time to pour the batter over the sausages and bake for 35–45 minutes.

Don't do what I sometimes can't resist doing and open the oven door to take a peek. Look only after about 30 minutes, or you risk your batter collapsing. I always serve my toad with boozy red wine onion gravy (see opposite), peas and mash.

Boozy Red Wine Onion Gravy

Smother your Yorkshire pudding with this rich, glossy, succulent and happily boozy gravy before stepping into comfort-food heaven.

SERVES 4
a good thick slice of butter (about 55g/2oz)
3 onions, peeled and thinly sliced
2 celery sticks, finely chopped
some fresh or dried rosemary, sage or thyme (if you like)
1 dsp plain flour
300ml (½ pint) red wine
salt and black pepper

Melt the butter in a heavy saucepan and fry the onion, celery and herbs really slowly; it should take at least 15 minutes. You want them to impart that lovely, sweet silkiness that onions have when treated right.

Stir in the flour and cook for a minute. Now add the wine, turn up the heat and let it bubble until the alcohol has burnt off. Simmer for about 5 minutes. If it looks thicker than you'd like, add a little water. Season to taste.

Easy-peasy Baked Beans

This is the speediest, tastiest, cheapest snack possible. If you have a lamb chop in the fridge it would be sublime grilled with plenty of rock salt and black pepper and served with these beauteous beans.

SERVES 1-2
olive or sunflower oil
1 onion, peeled and finely chopped
1 garlic clove, peeled and chopped
1 dsp curry paste (I use Patak's)
400g (14oz) can baked beans
1 tbsp chopped fresh coriander

In a small, heavy-bottomed pan heat a tablespoon or so of oil. Throw in the onion and cook gently until translucent. Then add the garlic and curry paste and fry for about a minute, stirring the whole time. Wait for the aroma of the spices to be released before pouring in the beans and heating through. Sprinkle with the fragrant coriander.

Mini Chicken Pies

Though I was young, free and single when I invented these little pies, they're now firm favourites with my girls ... and my dad (but that's a secret, as he's not allowed, under any circumstances, to indulge in all-butter pastry).

MAKES 6
400g (14oz) ready-rolled, all-butter puff pastry
25g (1oz) butter
½ onion, peeled and finely chopped
1 heaped tbsp plain flour
300ml (½ pint) milk
a good pinch dried thyme or a few sprigs fresh thyme
1 bay leaf
salt and black pepper
200–225g (7–8oz) cooked chicken, cut into chunky pieces
85g (3oz) frozen or fresh podded peas
1 tbsp chopped fresh parsley

Preheat the oven to 200°C/gas mark 6.

I use muffin tins to make these little babies, as they make really nice individual deep pies which the children love! I just whack the whole sheet of pastry over the tray, then gently press into the moulds. Then cut round the edges, leaving some spare pastry to fold over. Save all the trimmings to make the tops. Pop them into the fridge until you're ready to fill them.

In a heavy-based pan, melt the butter and gently fry the onion until transparent. Add the flour and stir for about 30 seconds. Pour in the milk, whisking all the time. Add the thyme, bay leaf and seasoning. Leave on a slow simmer for about 5–7 minutes (you want the flour to cook enough so that you can't taste it). Stir it every now and again.

Let the sauce cool down a little, then add the chicken, peas and parsley. Put a couple of tbsp of the chicken-and-veg jumble into each pie. Now roll out the remaining pastry and cut into rounds as lids. With a pastry brush, wet the edges and then stick them down over the filled bases.

Pop into the oven and bake for 20–30 minutes until golden. I usually serve these with creamy mash and my buttery carrots (see page 76).

Sandwiched Between a Rock and a Hard Place

As a struggling young actress I would often have to take temporary work to pay the bills. It was a hand-to-mouth existence and one was (to make sense of this story's title quickly) often caught between a rock and a hard place. 'One' always wanted to hone and perfect 'one's' craft as an actor, and yet 'one' was prevented from doing so by the need to earn 'oneself' a living. (You'll have noted that as a young and ambitious actress, 'one' always referred to oneself as 'one' – not me or I – it was all part of the method, darling!)

Anyway, after a particularly mind-numbing three-week stint spent stuffing (and licking!) thousands of envelopes in the dullest, greyest office imaginable (nursing countless zigzag paper cuts on my tongue), I decided I was going to change my luck and become my own boss so I could control my own destiny. How? By embracing one of my lifelong passions … No, not Shakespeare … Sandwiches. Aha! The role of sandwiches in my early acting career is a very well-guarded secret …

Within two days of this brainwave I kissed goodbye to licking and sticking envelopes and armed myself with a huge basket, a hand-written menu listing the most divine sandwiches South London had ever seen and a comfy pair of walking shoes.

Yep, for the next year, this little self-starter was beaten up every morning at six by her alarm clock before dragging herself into the kitchen to make sarnies. From the outset I took great pride in my work and wanted everything to be freshly made. So those early mornings were spent busily roasting chickens (they must have been the only chicken sandwiches in the country made with chicken roasted that very morning), making my own mayonnaise, chopping fresh salad and (though I can't believe this now) I even made some of the bread I used. I was 100 per cent dedicated to my new-found way of earning a living.

With a commitment to fresh ingredients and really caring that my sandwiches tasted good, it was no wonder that queues would already be forming as I got off the bus at Streatham Common. Yes, I ran my business alongside a bus stop!

Within just a few weeks business was booming and I was soon selling my gourmet sandwiches to shop assistants, traffic wardens (I needed the money!), shoppers, office workers, roadsweepers, the hairdressers on the corner just by Sainsbury's, the occasional policeman and sometimes passing taxi drivers.

So, even now, when I fear that my presenting career may be over and no one will buy this book, I can, if push comes to shove, always return to my very first business plan. All I'll need is a bus pass and a bus stop …

Here are just a few of the favourites with which the locals in Streatham Common fell in love. I'm not going to give exact weights and measures for the ingredients because I think the best sandwiches are made to personal taste. In fact, in my mind, the way in which a person makes a sandwich is the most revealing expression of their personality. Whereas many women judge men by the shoes they wear, or decide on friendships based on sense of humour, I make most of my assessments on the way people make their sandwiches. For me, a sandwich is like a self-portrait.

The Superwich

I named this sandwich because not only is it incredibly healthy but it's also incredibly delicious. It's 'super'! This is one of my favourite breakfasts, and I always have an energy-filled day whenever I take the time to treat myself to one.

pitta bread (see page 136), or a good brown bread (far healthier)
Grey Poupon French mustard, or any other good French mustard
a wee bit of mayonnaise, or a huge dollop!
avocado
alfalfa sprouts
watercress
tomatoes
a sprinkle toasted sesame seeds
salt and black pepper

Spread the bread with the mustard and mayo, then simply pile on the other ingredients. Don't forget to season well. Devour. The world had better be ready for your super powers once you've consumed this!

Marmite and Avocado Sandwich (The 'Mar-cado')

I think the deliciously dark colour and deep flavour of rye bread goes brilliantly with avocado but, of course, use any kind of bread you like. Don't be frightened by this combination: the sweet nuttiness of the avocado with the savouriness of the Marmite is deeply satisfying — unless, of course, you're from the 'I hate Marmite' brigade, in which case move straight on to my *next* suggestion!

PER PERSON
Marmite
butter
2 thin slices rye bread
1 avocado, peeled, stoned and mashed

I actually mix my Marmite into the butter and then slather it on to the bread before spreading the mashed 'avo' all over it. Oh dear, I'm going to have to go and make one now — I'm starving!

Mediterranean Tuna Sandwich

When I have the time, I like to chargrill my bread after drizzling olive oil on to it. Sometimes I rub a garlic clove all over it first too. What a little devil I am!

SERVES 2
2 red peppers, blackened (if possible)
a can tuna in oil
stoned black olives, chopped
fresh basil
lemon juice
black pepper
olive oil
peeled garlic for rubbing
4 slices sourdough or ciabatta bread

First blacken the peppers either by grilling them or, if you have a gas cooker, by placing them directly over the gas rings. If you don't have time, leave them raw: it will still be delicious, just different.

Put the tuna into a bowl and add the chopped peppers, olives, basil, a squeeze of lemon juice and some black pepper, and give it all a good stir. Drizzle olive oil on the bread, grill if you wish, then rub the garlic clove all over. Pile on the tuna mixture.

The Three Cs Sarnie *(Cheese, Coleslaw and Crisps)*

I feel no shame about this whatsoever: it's absolutely, shamelessly, bloody delicious.

PER PERSON
shop-bought coleslaw, or make your own using my mayonnaise
   (page 235)
whiter-than-white bread (the stuff that is like eating a duvet)
Cheddar or Red Leicester
Walker's cheese-and-onion crisps

Spoon the coleslaw over the bread, add thick slices of cheese and plenty of cheese-and-onion crisps. Put another slice of bread on top and press down lightly until you hear the crunch. *Yum!*

The FNJ (Figgy-nutty-jammy) Brioche

This really is one of the most fabulously Arabic answers to that North American classic, the peanut butter and jello sandwich. The fig jam is just divine, whilst the presence of lightly toasted almonds makes it sparkle. When I created this I would, in true actor mode, stand beside my mother's fridge with the door open, pretending I had just rustled it up. In my mind, the fridge was an enormous American fridge and my life was that of an LA superstar. Once eaten, I would slowly return to Streatham-based reality.

PER PERSON
fig jam (from Middle Eastern shops)
2 slices brioche, lightly toasted
flaked almonds, toasted

Simply spread the jam over the toasted brioche and sprinkle with the toasted almonds. Mmm, naughty!

Halwa (The Sweetest Sandwich in the World)

When we were kids, halwa (more commonly known as halva) was a real treat. It's made with super-healthy tahini (sesame-seed paste) but also tons of sugar. To counteract this, my dad would make us halwa sandwiches with wholemeal bread and always accompanied by a crunchy apple 'to clean the teeth from the sugar'. Though I'm not at all sure how sound his philosophy was, it made him feel better and did nothing to dent our enthusiasm for this super-sweet sarnie.

PER PERSON
2 slices brown bread, lightly buttered
2–3 thick slices halwa, enough to cover the bread
   (I like the one studded with pistachio nuts)
1 crispy apple

Queen of the chompers!

Julia's Raw-food Recipes

I love my sickeningly super-fit sister. Let me rephrase that. I love her *and* I hate her! This (her favourite quote) will tell you why: 'Let your food be your medicine, and your medicine be your food' (Hippocrates).

My sister Julia is a passionate advocate of raw-food living and has the most extraordinary levels of what I would call 'self-control'. Julia would argue that self-control has nothing to do with it, 'as it nourishes mind, body and spirit, giving me the energy of a two-year-old'. You see, not much passes her lips that isn't going to do something pretty extraordinary to her body. The higgledy-piggledy shelves in her beautiful country kitchen are filled with a breathtaking array of the weirdest and most wonderful super-healthy, super-duper foods.

Julia – wonder woman!

Pride of place, slap bang in the middle of her shelves, there is always a huge bottle of agave syrup, because, as Julia says, 'It has literally changed my life because I can use it without guilt'. It's apparently a sweet alternative to honey or maple syrup that doesn't give you the same 'dangerous' highs and lows that sugar does (I personally quite like those dangerous highs and lows).

Another of her favourite super-foods is bee pollen ('crunchy little bits of joy'), which she adds to her cereal for its amazing youth-giving qualities. Then there are cacao nibs. Apparently you have to be very careful with these babies as they can give you 'scary amounts of energy that will literally keep you up all night' (sounds brilliant to me).

The real frustration with not being able to tempt her away from her strict dietary regime is of course principally to do with my own shameful jealousy, because, you see, my lovely sister's hair shines, her skin blooms, her eyes sparkle – even her bones (which you can't see) look gorgeous! But this isn't all. On top of her fabulous looks, she can also chop wood like a bloke, carry bags of coal on her back, hike for miles and still have the energy to scrub the house (she's Virgoan) from top to bottom and (wait for it) iron her tea-towels, her sheets *and*, unbelievably, her bathmat. I mean who in their right mind irons the bathmat? I swear it's not easy being Julia's sister …

So, here are her favourite raw-food recipes. Please feel free to try them … I won't feel at all threatened … honestly!

Last month, driving us home after staying with Julia for a week, my husband remarked with great seriousness, 'Sweetheart, I'm so pleased I married *you*.'

'What do you mean?' I asked.

'I just couldn't imagine a life of cacao nibs, agave syrup and bee pollen …' It was the most serious I've seen my husband in months.

Live Raw Soup *(Yes, Raw Soup!)*

OK. For this, I'm handing you over to my little, but incredibly fit (in all ways), sister Julia!

SERVES 1 HUNGRY PERSON
2 carrots
2 sticks celery
1 courgette
600ml (1 pint) boiled water
1–2 tsp vegetable stock powder, tamari sauce
   or Braggs liquid amino
fresh coriander leaves

I usually use a variety of vegetables. Except parsnips – I find these a bit hard to digest raw.

Chop the vegetables. Add the veg stock powder, or tamari or liquid amino, depending on how healthy you want to be, to the boiling water and stir.

Put the raw vegetables in a powerful blender with the water mixture. I have a Vitamix, which is the equivalent of having a small jet plane in your kitchen. I highly recommend investing in one: it makes the most beautiful smoothies and nut milk, and can blend a mobile phone really well if you ever feel the urge to accidentally drop one in!

You can add whatever herbs take your fancy, even a little raw garlic, but only a little, otherwise it can overpower the delicate taste of the vegetables. And that's it! You have a hot soup, but are eating the vegetables raw, which means you haven't killed any of the essential minerals and vitamins that are destroyed in cooking and, yes, even steaming. You're literally eating live food.

Bliss Balls

Let me hand you over to Julia again: she calls these bliss balls because they're utterly delicious and give her the power, energy and focus needed for chopping wood!

MAKES 20–30
350g (12oz) strawberries
100g (3½oz) cacao powder
100ml (3½ fl. oz) orange juice
100g (3½oz) shelled hemp seeds
60g (2¼oz) coconut butter or 100g (3½oz) cacao butter
50g (1¾oz) goji berries, soaked in water for 20 minutes, then drained
50g (1¾oz) stoned dates, finely chopped
4 tbsp desiccated coconut
Optional extras
lecuma powder
maca powder
cacao nibs
raw almonds, soaked in water overnight, then drained

Blend all the ingredients (except the coconut) in a food processor.

Transfer the mixture to a suitable container and leave in the fridge overnight, or freezer for a few hours, then shape into walnut-sized balls and roll in the coconut.

A Poor Man's Dish Fit for a King

My cousin Elias is an astonishingly healthy man and looks at least twenty years younger than his sixty years. This simple fact *can* cause the green-eyed monster to visit the far less disciplined men in the family.

For years, every single morning he has drunk an eggcup full of olive oil (yep, on an empty stomach). This gives him not only his Samson-like locks (again, something that has never gone down too well with the more, shall we say, follically challenged men in the family) but also his perfectly smooth, unlined skin.

There's always been a fair amount of scepticism from the male relations about Elias's lifestyle choices. In fact, when he first converted to vegetarianism he received countless letters from friends and relatives in Jordan sending their heartfelt condolences and moving messages of hope, urging him, 'Not to worry, one day soon you will almost certainly recover'!

But Elias is a man of discipline. He lives just round the corner and it's rare to be out and about without seeing him running or cycling like a man possessed. In fact, he is so committed to the great outdoors (of SE19), I'm convinced I once saw him hang-gliding over Streatham Common, though he fiercely denies it.

I remember, as a child, being awestruck by his stories of the weird and wonderful fasts he would go on. In retrospect, I was probably more dumbstruck than awestruck. I mean, how on earth can anyone *not* eat for longer than 3 hours? For instance, one of his more extreme fasts involved him running every day for at least 2 hours and eating only grass shoots and water. Apparently by the fourth week (yup, the *fourth week*) he said he felt so light in mind, body and spirit that when he next went for a long jog it was as though he had wings on his trainers. I didn't have the heart to suggest he was possibly hallucinating and that anyone would feel light in body (and absent in mind) if they only ate flaming grass shoots!

Now whatever you do, don't let his eccentricities put you off the next recipe, because when Elias is *not* on a fast he's not only a voracious eater, but, most notably, a very good cook. He's a bit of a Percy Thrower too, and his allotment (with all its deliciously exotic fruit and veg), is like a small verdant corner of Jordan, nestled in the heart of Streatham. There aren't many people who can grow a prize-sized watermelon in SE19 but I'm telling you, my cousin Elias is one of them.

Anyway, enough of this praise — it will only cause even more jealousy amongst the ranks of family men. So let me instead turn your attention to a dish that is popular all over the Middle East and is one of Elias's favourites.

Elias and I have an agreement —
he supplies me with watermelons
and I supply him with baklava!

Mejeddarah

Mejedderah is a humble pleasure of a dish, consisting of fragrant basmati rice, brown lentils and masses of fried onions gently spiced with cumin and black pepper. In our family, we serve it with a chunky tomato and cucumber salad and thick, creamy yogurt, possibly making it one of the healthiest dishes in this book, especially if you eat it, and only it, once a day, straight after running uphill backwards for 3 hours (which I swear I've seen Elias do).

It's really important for this dish that you have a good heavy-bottomed pan with a tightly fitting lid, otherwise the rice and lentils will burn and there will be no saving them!

SERVES 4

125g (4½oz) brown lentils, washed
2 onions, peeled and chopped, plus another 4 onions,
    peeled and sliced
1 tsp each ground cumin and ground cinnamon
plenty of salt and black pepper
6–7 tbsp olive oil
150g (5½oz) basmati rice
a pinch granulated sugar

Put the lentils in a pan with 250ml (9 fl. oz) water, bring to the boil, then turn down the heat and cook them until almost tender and the water has been absorbed: about 20–30 minutes. Add more water if they start to dry out.

Meanwhile, gently fry the chopped onions and spices, along with a generous ½ tsp black pepper (I usually use more), in 2 tbsp olive oil. When the onions are a deep golden brown, mix with the rice and add some salt and pepper.

Once the lentils are cooked, add the rice and onion mixture and pour in water until it's about 1cm (½in) above the top of the rice. Check the seasoning, then cover with a tight-fitting lid and cook on a really low heat for about 15 minutes, until small holes begin to appear in the surface of the rice and the rice is tender.

Meanwhile, in a large frying pan heat 4–5 tbsp oil until it's nice and hot. Fry the sliced onions for a few minutes before turning the heat down a bit. Now sprinkle them with sugar and cook until they're dark brown.

Turn the rice and lentils into a bowl and top with the fried onions.

A Bad Case of the Falafels!

Whatever you do, *don't ignore this recipe*! If there's only one recipe you do in this book, do this one!

If you've only ever tasted those bullet-like falafels that British supermarkets have on offer, I beg of you to wipe all memory of them from your minds. When I asked my husband if he liked falafels, he thought I was referring to one of two things: (a) a small town in Cyprus (in which case it was probably yes, because he likes Cyprus), or (b) those nasty balls of mushed-up papier mâché you get at music festivals (in which case it was no).

Even good supermarket falafels bear absolutely no relation whatsoever to what my father calls 'a true falafel'. True falafels *have* to be gloriously spicy with a crispy-on-the-outside crunch, and a light-and-fluffy-on-the-inside bit-of-give. Believe me, my dad knows what he's talking about when it comes to falafels, and there's absolutely no calming him down on the few occasions he's had a Bad Case of the Falafels!

As a boy he attended the Bishops' School, an all-boys' establishment in the middle of bustling downtown Amman. He has many fond memories of his time there, not least because of the falafels that were on offer, without fail, every break time. (Sure beats a bottle of warm milk in a wet playground in Streatham.)

To this day, he often waxes lyrical about Youssef, a skinny, bent-double Egyptian chap, who looked about ninety (though Dad says he was probably not a day over thirty-five) and would bring his decrepit donkey and cart to the school most days. With all the wiliness of the Pied Piper, followed by hungry children all circling and dancing round him, he'd park slap bang in the centre of the playground (if only ice-cream vans had once done the same in South London). In his own time, Youssef would light up his coal fire and begin to fry, eventually croaking, 'Falafels! Just one piastre [about 5p]. Come and get your falafels, you little bastards!' Youssef had a bit of a love-hate relationship with his youthful clientele.

My father says that what unfolded was a scene of extreme falafel fanaticism. Whilst a great many *true* falafels were eaten with great eagerness and hungry zeal, there were often occasions when the odd burnt one would soar through the sky, only to bounce off Youssef's rather large hooked nose. Usually at this point all the children would run and scream, 'Youssef! You have a bad case of the falafels!' Youssef was absolutely right — little bastards, the lot of them!

Believe me, I did a *lot* of research whilst creating this recipe and I can now say with great pride that it produces the best falafels *I* have ever tasted. For me it was a very important and defining moment when, after he tried them for the first time, my father announced, 'My dear, these are the truest falafels I have ever eaten.' Now *that* made me a very happy cook indeed!

Dad (right), Auntie Jamileh and their elder brother Fasid, scrubbed and polished within an inch of their lives!

True Falafels

In our household, the name of this lovely dish has now become a synonym for when things go wrong in the kitchen. This quick story is an example of how, last Christmas, I was well and truly falafelled!

My raw-food, vegan sister Julia only ever makes an exception to her rigid diet on Christmas Day, allowing herself roast potatoes and parsnips. Bless her. She really looks forward to this 'indulgence' and it's such a key part of her culinary calendar that she actually starts salivating around Easter. I also love (even if it's just once a year) to make her eat something that *isn't* raw. But last Christmas — oh dear. I really screwed up, cooking her potatoes and parsnips with ours … in duck fat! She actually cried and, I have to be honest, so did I. Mark thought there'd been a tragedy, until it slowly dawned on him, 'Oh dear, you've both been falafelled.' Being a sensible specimen of maleness, he knew this was far worse than any ordinary tragedy and immediately adopted a very low profile. Poor Julia.

She spent the next two days on the phone telling all her vegan and vegetarian friends about my unforgivable faux pas, and they between them decided that my penance should be to hold a falafel party for them all. There were eight of them and they all ordered a minimum of ten each. I'll leave the maths to you!

SERVES 4–6
175g (6oz) dried chickpeas, soaked in cold water for 24 hours
85g (3oz) dried fava beans, soaked in cold water for 24 hours
a handful each fresh parsley and coriander leaves
2 tsp each ground coriander, ground cumin and ground cinnamon
1 tsp ground allspice
1½ tsp each salt and freshly ground black pepper
1 tsp cayenne pepper (optional)
2 garlic cloves, peeled
1 tsp bicarbonate of soda (this gives a lovely lightness to the falafels)
¼ green pepper, seeded and very, very finely chopped
2 tbsp flour
3 tbsp sesame seeds
groundnut oil, for deep frying

Drain the chickpeas and fava beans.

Chop the parsley and coriander, then put into a blender and whizz until fine. Add the chickpeas, fava beans, spices, garlic, baking soda, green pepper and flour, and blend again to a smooth paste.

Stir in the sesame seeds. Leave to rest for about an hour in the fridge.

When you're ready to eat, gently bring the oil up to heat in a deep-fat frying pan. To test if it's hot enough, put in a tiny bit of the mixture: if it sizzles, it's time. Gently take 1 tbsp mixture at a time, drop as many as you can into the oil without overcrowding and wait till they float to the top, then gently turn them over. Fry for a couple of minutes until golden brown, then drain on kitchen paper. Serve with pitta bread (see page 136), tahini sauce (see page 122), pickles and maybe even some of my harissa (see page 202).

Obviously fashion wasn't a priority on this holiday!

Super Suppers

Going Down the Pork Chops (Shops)

When I played the ball-breaking Annie Palmer in *EastEnders*, the strangest thing would sometimes happen to me in supermarkets. As I glided seamlessly from the deli counter via the meat counter to the vodka counter (if only!), I'd become increasingly aware of this ever-growing gaggle of shoppers all congregating at the end of whatever aisle I found myself in. Going shopping at that time was a little like being the Pied Piper of Croydon, except rather than children following the sound of my music, it was shoppers following the contents of my shopping basket! Around the time I was passing through the slimline-tonic aisle, someone would usually have plucked up the courage to come up to me and say something like, 'What are *you* doing in *here*?' as if no one off the telly should ever do their own shopping.

On one occasion, I vividly remember a woman at the meat counter sidling up to me and seeming particularly put out by the fact that I was shopping 'normally'. Then, in the middle of telling me how she thought I would have had 'someone else to do this sort of thing', she stopped suddenly, having spotted what was in my basket: a large pot of luscious cream, thick juicy organic pork chops, fragrant saffron, a bottle of smoky dry sherry, a jar of golden Dijon mustard and some pert spring onions. Her eyes darted back to my face and she gave me a conspiratorial look, whispering, 'Oh, I see,' as though she had had all her questions on the meaning of life immediately answered. 'It's all very *posh*.' As she raised her left eyebrow, in an instant I realized I'd been forgiven for being somewhere I shouldn't have been. Somehow, I had confirmed either her worst or her best preconceptions (I still can't work out which) about those people 'off the telly'.

Posh Pork Chops

Well, here's the super-easy dish I was shopping for. It's a great recipe for busy people who love making good home-made suppers. So, this is dedicated to that woman at the meat counter, who, in all honesty, probably thought I had my own chef waiting for me at home. Oh, the glamour of it all ...

If you fancy, try this with rabbit, it goes ever so well. Just brown the rabbit in some olive oil and then simmer it in the stock and sherry for about an hour before adding the cream and mustard. Chicken works really well too.

SERVES 4
vegetable oil
4 pork chops, flattened with a rolling pin (roll with love, not rage)
butter
a large bunch spring onions, cut into strips
2 large carrots, peeled and cut into batons
20 small mushrooms
1 glass sherry
1 tsp grated ginger
300ml (½ pint) chicken stock, hot
salt and black pepper
3 large tbsp Dijon mustard (only Grey Poupon will do,
    and I know it sounds a lot, but it's not)
1 tsp arrowroot, mixed with 2 tbsp cold water
300ml (½ pint) double cream

Heat your oil in a heavy frying pan and brown the chops on both sides (make sure they're really dry first to avoid spitting). Don't move them about too much. Cook through for 5–10 minutes, depending on thickness.

Whilst they're cooking, put a large knob of butter into a heavy casserole and add the spring onions, carrots and mushrooms. Add the sherry and let it bubble until reduced by half. Add the ginger, hot chicken stock, salt and pepper, and simmer without a lid for 5 minutes until the vegetables are tender.

Take out the vegetables and set aside. Add the mustard and arrowroot mixture to the liquid in the pan, turn up the heat and stir with a whisk until thickened. Turn down the heat and continue whisking as you pour in the cream. Put the vegetables back into the sauce and stir.

Place the chops on warm plates and pour the sauce over the top. This is perfect served with rice and pretty peas à la franglaise (see page 78).

A Passport to Sunny Food

An out-of-work actor is not a pretty sight and when I decided to leave *EastEnders* (which I'd been in for two and a half years) I was (a) petrified I'd never work again, and (b) terrified I'd be forever known as 'that 'orrible Annie Palmer off the telly'.

Everyone, from producers to agents, canteen ladies to my aunties and uncles, had warned me that it can take years to shake off a soap character, so I was prepared for rather a lot of 'out-of-work resting' after I left Boreham Wood studios for the last time. Luckily, as it turned out, I actually got very *little* rest.

Within a week of leaving Walford Square (in the obligatory black cab), I was immediately cast as a 'loose woman' for a brand-new ITV series of the same name: a brilliantly simple concept where a group of 'witty, articulate, ballsy birds' (not my words) sit in a studio and 'discuss' whatever takes their fancy. Unbelievable, really, that we got paid for it!

I had the time of my life, and, thanks to the brilliant anchor host, Kaye Adams, I received a crash course in becoming a TV presenter. Ironically, it was whilst appearing on *Loose Women* that I was spotted by the producer of a BBC show called *Passport to the Sun*. Within a matter of weeks I was asked to do it, and so found myself on the payroll for both nattering with other women *and* travelling out to Majorca. How could I refuse? And the rest, as they say, is history. Apart from pausing to have my daughters, I have been presenting — almost exclusively for the BBC — for the past ten years.

For most of those years I've spent the summer in Spain, filming a variety of different 'sun' programmes. If I had a pound for every time a member of the public shouts out at me, 'Some people get all the luck,' I'd be rich beyond my wildest dreams. But in actual fact, as anyone who does location filming will tell you, not only does it involve some very, very long hours in the stifling heat, often feeling very homesick, but also, everywhere you go, *other* people are jumping into swimming pools, lounging on sun-drenched beaches and indulging in long lunches.

I know you're probably thinking, 'Yeah, yeah, stop moaning,' but honestly, it was tough! However, one of the best bits of being away was, of course, the food. I simply fell in love with Spanish cuisine and I especially became a real sucker for tapas, which were perfectly designed for those 20-minute breaks between takes. Needless to say, I can consume the contents of an awful lot of plates of tapas in just 20 minutes!

The first time I had this next dish was at the end of quite possibly the worst filming day of the first series of *Passport to the Sun*. The director had literally begged me to do an insane bungee jump, which he was convinced would make great viewing (and would also win him some brownie points with the producer). Well, eventually, very much against my will, I agreed to do it — and it was everything I feared it would be. Having been bounced towards all four corners of Majorca's coastline, when I finally landed with a painful bump I was so utterly petrified, so pumped up with adrenalin and an extraordinary amount of rage, that I'm ashamed to say I attacked the poor director, raining him with punches.

Mortified, and nervous that he might have a mutiny on his hands, as a means of appeasement he took myself and the crew (the poor cameraman had had to bungee jump too) out for a conciliatory dinner. It worked. My fists ceased their assault and we all cheered up considerably at the thought of food. Ten minutes later we were ensconced in a gorgeous tapas bar by the sea and as the sun set over our now very merry table, we indulged in plate after plate of the most fantastic tapas. We ate and drank until we could no longer feel the pain (although my bloodshot eyes from the whiplash did present us with an enormous continuity dilemma!).

Gloriously Sticky, Garlicky, Spanish-style Chicken

I *have* tinkered with this recipe a fair bit in order to try to re-create the exact flavour I remember. So, here's *the* perfect Spanish chicken dish, which simply must be eaten whenever you find yourself forced to do a bungee jump against your will.

SERVES 4–6
about 3 tbsp plain flour
salt and black pepper
smoked paprika
1 small chicken (ask your butcher to chop
   it into bite-sized pieces on the bone)
150ml (5 fl. oz) olive oil
20 garlic cloves, unpeeled
200ml (7 fl. oz) sherry
fresh parsley, chopped

Season the flour well with salt, pepper and paprika, then roll the chicken pieces in it.

Heat the oil in a heavy pan. Once it's hot, turn the heat down and gently fry the chicken until cooked through: about 6–10 minutes. Don't overcrowd the pan: you might have to do it in more than one batch.

Now fry the garlic, skins and all, with the chicken until light golden brown. Remove from the heat and add the sherry slowly. Then gradually turn up the heat to burn off the alcohol. Turn the heat down again and simmer nice and slowly until the sherry has disappeared, which will leave you with the tastiest oil ever.

Leave it all to cool (if you can bear to), sprinkle with parsley, then eat it with your fingers. It goes without saying that all those delicious juices simply must be mopped up with some gorgeously rustic bread. Aah, I love it.

Feeding the Troops

As I said at the beginning, taking part in *Celebrity MasterChef* was an utterly terrifying experience from start to finish. Imagine stepping into a relentless whirlwind of repeatedly more stressful challenges, all designed to reduce us so-called 'celebs' to quivering wrecks. Any of us with aspirations to being considered C-listers were reduced to capital Z-listers once Gregg Wallace and John Torode had finished with us.

Add to this already potent recipe for stress the fact that I was also a good three months pregnant with my second daughter, and my raging hormones were really managing to ratchet up the drama for me!

So when, after a long day's filming in the unbelievably pressurized atmosphere of a professional kitchen, we were told that at the crack of dawn (5 a.m.) next day we would be cooking for the army, in an outside kitchen, in the freezing cold, I went into serious meltdown. This was the point at which I fully felt I'd bitten off more than I could chew.

Gregg's and John's challenge for us was to create the kind of food that fifty young cadets would *want* to eat after 4 hours of manoeuvres on a freezing cold battlefield. Crikey! I went straight into panic mode. What on earth do young cadets eat? Shepherd's pie? (No, all kids hate shepherd's pie.) Macaroni cheese? (What if they don't like cheese? Won't it remind them of school dinners?) I know! Sausage and mash. (But no, I'll never have the time, or the muscle power, to make the mash smooth and creamy for fifty cadets.) Increasingly desperate, I entertained toad-in-the-hole. (Come on, Nadia, get real. Batter for fifty?)

Hang on a minute! I do actually cook for my own troop of teenage nephews and stepdaughters all the time. Wrack your brains, Nadia! What do they love? Yes, that's it! My brood's voices started to ricochet round my head, a slowly growing chorus building and building … 'Nanna's balls,' it said. 'Nanna's balls.' Of course! Nanna's balls. Yes, I had it! 'Nanna' being the kids' nickname for me and my balls, of course, referring to my meatballs. 'Nanna's balls' simply makes the kids fall off their chairs with laughter – so that was it. I'd found my culinary weapon. And guess what? I won the round with a stonking majority!

Nanna's Balls

Sometimes 'my crowd' demands rice instead of pasta with these flavoursome little dynamos, and it works really well. Be careful that you don't get any of the pith when you zest the lemon, as it spoils the flavour. If you fancy, use pork instead of beef, or even half and half.

SERVES 4–6

For the meatballs
500g (1lb 2oz) top-quality minced beef
6–7 tbsp milk
1 thick slice white bread, no crusts, made into breadcrumbs
5 tbsp chopped fresh parsley
finely grated zest of 1 large lemon
2 garlic cloves, peeled and minced (optional)
1 medium onion, peeled and grated
55g (2oz) Parmesan, freshly grated
1 egg, beaten
a little olive oil and butter (optional)
For the sauce
3 tbsp olive oil
2 large tbsp tomato purée
2 x 400g (14oz) cans chopped tomatoes
2 tbsp water

A restaurant we found in Marrakech. If it all goes tits up I've got somewhere to go!

Put all the meatball ingredients, apart from the oil and butter, into your favourite bowl. Now get mucky by thoroughly combining it all with your hands, then rolling the mixture into walnut-sized balls.

If you're in true cheffy mode, gently fry the balls in a little oil and butter, turning them until they're browned all over. Or, if you're in a 'very busy, can't be bothered' mood, throw them into a hot oven – 200°C/gas mark 6 – for 10 minutes until brown, turning once.

Meanwhile, for the sauce, gently heat the olive oil in a frying pan, then add the tomato purée and fry until the purée warms through and the smell changes to that of fried tomatoes. Add the tomatoes and water. Bring up to a bubble, then turn down to a simmer for 20–25 minutes.

Add the meatballs to their tomato sauce right at the end so that they simply heat through; any more cooking will toughen them. If the sauce has reduced a bit too much, add a little more water.

Serve with rice or pasta and sprinkle with some more grated Parmesan; make sure it's *freshly* grated in order to avoid cries of 'Yuk! I can smell sick!'

Creamy Mushrooms on Toast

Creamy mushrooms flavoured with garlic, shallots and parsley, spooned on to perfectly crusty, buttery white bread. Mmmm. This is my and Mark's curl-up-on-the-sofa dish of choice.

SERVES 4
butter
olive oil
3 garlic cloves, peeled and finely chopped
450g (1lb) your favourite mushrooms, quartered
2 shallots, peeled and finely chopped
2 tbsp chopped fresh parsley
salt and lots of black pepper
4 slices good crusty white bread

Heat 55g (2oz) butter and 2 tbsp oil in a large, heavy frying pan. When the foam subsides, add the garlic and fry slowly until softened: be careful you don't burn it (if you do burn it, start again, as the flavour will be ruined).

If you need to, add some more oil and, when it's hot, add the mushrooms, being careful not to overcrowd the pan; you will probably have to do them in two or three batches. Fry the mushrooms, swirling the pan so that they brown evenly. Now the mushrooms need a little time alone, so take them out, with the garlic, and put to one side.

In a little more oil, fry the shallots slowly until they're tender. Once they're cooked, throw in the parsley, garlic and mushrooms. Season well with salt and plenty of black pepper (mushrooms love black pepper).

Keep everything warm while you toast the bread. Spread the toast with plenty of butter (this could be garlic butter if you haven't got to go anywhere later in the day), then pour the mushrooms and their juices on to the toast.

Fake Wiener Schnitzel

Fake because, of course, this dish is traditionally made with veal.
I use organic, free-range pork instead, so I can sleep at night!

SERVES 4
4 pork escalopes
about 3 tbsp plain flour
salt and black pepper
1 egg, beaten
50g dried breadcrumbs
3 tbsp sesame seeds
juice of ½ lemon
groundnut oil

Put the escalopes into a plastic bag and bash them out with a rolling pin
until they're really thin. If you've had a row, this is very therapeutic.

Put the seasoned flour on one plate, the egg on another and the
breadcrumbs mixed with sesame seeds on a third. Squeeze a little lemon
juice on to the escalopes, then dip them into the flour. Next dip them in
the egg and finally in the breadcrumbs and sesame seeds. Place in the fridge
for 30 minutes.

Heat enough oil in a heavy frying pan to shallow fry. It is hot enough
when you throw in a little flour and it sizzles. Now slip the escalopes in.
Fry on both sides until crisp and golden on the outside and cooked through
on the inside: this should take 3–8 minutes, depending on the thickness
of your pork. Then drain on a piece of kitchen paper.

I love to serve this with a mixed salad, some lemon to squeeze and simple
buttered flat noodles. Oh, and a sprinkle of parsley if I have some.

Fennel and Tomato with Smoky Lardons

I remember, when I was nine, having my friend Veronica Lake round to tea. Mum had made a gorgeous fennel dish, which she served alongside a huge leg of roast lamb and garlic-kissed roast potatoes. I couldn't wait for Veronica to tuck in so she could tell me how brilliant my mum was. But suddenly, she ran out of the kitchen in tears, mumbling about garlic being foreign. So, if by some mad chance you are reading this, Ronnie, it's still not too late to give it a try — go *onnn*!

SERVES 4
2 large fennel bulbs
olive oil
125g (4½oz) bacon lardons
1 medium onion, peeled and thinly sliced
2 garlic cloves, peeled and chopped
1 tsp fennel seeds
2 tsp tomato purée
400g (14oz) can chopped tomatoes
salt and black pepper
For the topping
6 tbsp fresh breadcrumbs
6 tbsp freshly grated Parmesan (please, not ready-grated –
    we all know what that tastes like!)
finely grated zest of 1 organic lemon
2 garlic cloves, peeled and very finely chopped

Preheat the oven to 180°C/gas mark 4.

Trim the tops off the fennel bulbs. Cut the bulbs into slices about 5mm (¼in) thick, removing the hard core at the bottom. Toss the slices in olive oil, then spread over an oven tray and bake for 15 minutes. Remove from the oven and turn the temperature up to 220°C/gas mark 7.

Fry the bacon until browned in a heavy 20–23cm (8–9in) pan that can go in the oven. Remove with a slotted spoon and set aside. Add 4 tbsp oil to the pan and sauté the onion and garlic for 3–4 minutes. Add the fennel and fry until browned.

While the fennel is frying, heat 2 tsp oil in a small–medium pan and fry the fennel seeds until they start to sizzle and pop; be careful they don't burn. Add the tomato purée and stir for 2 minutes. Pour in the tomatoes, season and then pour this mixture over the fried fennel.

Mix the topping ingredients together and sprinkle over the fennel. Bake until very crisp: about 20–30 minutes.

Rice with Meat and Chickpeas (*Ssshh — and Harissa*)

My family use only water in this dish ('that is the way it has always been done') and of course it's lovely, but dare I say it, I prefer to use a good stock for an extra layer of flavour. The rebel in me also drives me to serve (and I have to keep this quiet) my fiery Moroccan harissa sauce with this meal, simply because I think it goes really well.

SERVES 4
25g (1oz) butter
2 tbsp olive oil
450g (1lb) leg of lamb, cut into 2.5cm (1in) cubes
450g (1lb) pickling onions, or small shallots, peeled
1 tsp each ground cumin and ground cinnamon
½ tsp ground turmeric
85g (3oz) dried chickpeas, soaked overnight in cold water
600ml (1 pint) lamb stock (or water)
1 tsp each salt and black pepper
275 g (10oz) long-grain rice, washed and drained
To serve
fresh parsley or coriander, chopped
harissa (see page 202)

Melt the butter and oil in a large saucepan. Add the lamb and cook until it's a rich brown: don't move it about too much. Remove and put to one side. Now add the whole onions to the pan and fry them until they're a lovely golden brown; keep your eyes on them, though, giving them a good stir here and there. Now add the spices and stir a couple of times.

Now it's time for the drained chickpeas to go in, as well as the sealed lamb. Add enough stock or water to cover everything. Make sure the water comes about 2.5cm (1in) over the ingredients. Bring to the boil, then turn down the heat and leave to bubble gently for about 1–1½ hours, or until the meat and chickpeas are really soft. Season well.

Then either add to the liquid or reduce it by boiling, so you end up with a couple of cups of liquid. Bring it up to the boil. Add the rice, check the seasoning, then simmer until the rice is cooked: about 15 minutes. Sometimes I have to add a bit more water if the rice isn't quite cooked.

Leave it to rest for a few minutes before piling it all into a serving dish and sprinkling with either parsley or coriander. Serve the harissa in a small bowl on the side.

Harissa — Spicy Chilli Sauce

I wear my washing-up gloves when I chop the chillies, as I've had some very unpleasant experiences when I haven't, as has Mark.

MAKES ABOUT 225G (8OZ)
175g (6oz) fresh red chillies
1 dsp tomato purée
4 tbsp canned pimento, chopped
4 garlic cloves, peeled
2 tsp each ground coriander and ground caraway seeds
1 tsp ground cumin
salt
1 dsp red wine vinegar
olive oil

Remove the seeds from the chillies if you don't want it too hot! Chop the chillies and pop into a blender (or pestle and mortar) with all the rest of the ingredients, adding a couple of glugs of olive oil. Blend until you have a smooth paste. Check the seasoning.

You can keep this in a jar in the fridge, but cover it with more olive oil to preserve it.

Cousin Nayef
in an apron –
he'll kill me
for printing it!

Showing Off in the Kitchen

Lunch, Camera, Action

As kids, we were incredibly lucky. My sisters and I used to have the most fabulous holidays, travelling to wherever my dad was working on a film – Egypt, Malta, Morocco and, one of my personal favourites (though perhaps the least exotic), Almeria in southern Spain.

When I travelled there at the ripe old age of ten, my father was acting in a film called *The Wind and the Lion*, starring Sean Connery and Candice Bergen and directed by John Milius. In it, Connery was playing an Arab sheikh and my father played his sidekick, Sharif Wazan. More importantly, and rather strangely, my father also doubled up as Sean Connery's voice coach.

Imagine! Being given the mission to equip possibly *the* most distinctive Scottish voice in cinema history with an Arabic accent? Well, after just a few days of trying, my father learned to accept that this particular sheikh was always going to have more than a wee Scottish twang. Though he admired Sean greatly, he would emerge from various location tents in the mock-desert worriedly muttering, 'I've been given an impossible task. Simply impossible!'

I felt incredibly grown up, swanning around set, chatting to actors, hanging out with the stunt guys and rooting through the huge costume trucks. In fact, I distinctly remember being bought a pair of Spanish cowboy boots (which in my mind's eye became my first high heels) and clumping around, truly believing that 007 would fall in love with me and marry me. OK – I *was* only ten!

But, more importantly, the other thing of which I have everlasting memories was … surprise, surprise … lunch!

Location catering on a big film is an impressive affair: incredible food prepared in fully kitted-out kitchens in big lorries.

I had been impressed with these culinary convoys on the sets of many of Dad's other films, so on about the third day in Spain, as a lovely surprise, he arranged for me to be allowed 'properly' into their world.

As I stepped into the Tardis-like vehicle, there was an immediate assault on all my senses. The sounds of pans crashing, meat frying, onions sizzling and chefs shouting were deafening. It looked and sounded like a film set in itself. I stood there with my eyes out on stalks, taking it all in, allowing it all to soak into my food DNA. Then my father, bless him, said to the catering team at the top of his voice, 'Your helper has arrived.' I held my breath in a mixture of disbelief and total nervous excitement …

All eyes turned to focus on the little girl in Spanish cowboy boots. The next thing I knew, I was up to my elbows in barbecued peppers, garlic and coriander, making the most gorgeous Mediterranean pepper salad you could possibly imagine! As I chopped, washed, mixed and grilled, I was truly in my element, daydreaming about the fact that 007 no less, the great Sean Connery, was about to taste and eat *my* very own chargrilled Mediterranean pepper salad. At that moment, aged ten, part of the kitchen crew, cooking with fervour, I knew the world was my oyster. Unfortunately, I never did become a Bond Girl …

I love this behind-the-scenes photo – it looks like a hundred years ago.

Typical, there's a picture of Julia but not of me, and my boots were better than hers!

Mediterranean Pepper Salad

The head chef on the catering bus was a very fierce Moroccan chap, hence the use of exotic spices. If you fancy a more Spanish flavour, omit the spices and swap the coriander for parsley.

SERVES 4

2 each green, red and yellow peppers
4 tbsp olive oil
1 small onion, peeled and very finely chopped
2–4 fat garlic cloves, peeled and finely chopped
¼ tsp each ground cinnamon, ground cumin and
    ground coriander
2 medium tomatoes, chopped into small cubes,
    or whatever takes your fancy
a handful finely chopped fresh coriander

First the peppers need to have their skins burned black all over – and I mean *burned black*. And, of course, the most delicious way to do this is on the barbecue. But let's assume, as is usually the case here in Blighty, that it's the middle of winter. In this case, you could either grill them or, if you have a gas cooker, place them directly over the gas rings. Once they're completely blackened, pop them into a large bowl and cover with cling film.

Meanwhile gently heat the oil in a frying pan, add the onion and garlic, and cook until translucent. Add the spices and fry until their aroma is released (about 30 seconds), then add the tomatoes and simmer gently for 5 minutes.

While the tomatoes are simmering, gently rub the skins off the peppers. Don't be too pernickety about this, because I think a few black bits here and there really add to the taste. And don't, whatever you do, be tempted to run them under the tap, because all the benefits earned from the burning will be annihilated. And don't get carried away with this and forget the tomatoes simmering on top of the stove!

Chop the peppers into the same shapes as you've made the tomatoes and add to the tomato mixture.

Put into a dish and throw on the chopped coriander leaves. This salad can be served warm or cold and goes particularly well with Dina's Moroccan chicken (see page 208).

Dina's Moroccan Chicken

As this is Dina's recipe I'm not going to argue … but I don't muck about washing and drying *my* rice!

Because of the way she cooks the chicken, the meat in this dish is ultra-soft and flavoursome. The spices really penetrate the meat, making it deeply aromatic, whilst the rice stuffing really is manna from heaven. You will never taste tastier rice — once you've indulged in it for the first time, it may well become your rice of choice. So long as you don't scrimp on the quality of olives, the rice will have a lovely, salty sourness.

The rice stuffing can easily be made in its own right, and if you use a vegetable stock it could be adopted by vegetarians.

SERVES 6–8
juice of 1 lemon
2 small chickens
ground turmeric
whole shelled almonds, fried in butter
For the stuffing
325g (11½oz) basmati rice
salt
a large knob butter
850ml (1½ pints) chicken stock
3–4 tsp ground turmeric
2 tsp each ground ginger and ground cumin
1 tsp sweet paprika
about 30 olives, stuffed with pimentos, quartered
a large bunch fresh coriander (and that means a large bunch,
   not one of those tiny supermarket packets), roughly chopped

Squeeze the lemon juice over the chickens, inside and out. Rub the chickens all over with turmeric. Set to one side.

For the stuffing, wash the rice first in hot and then in cold water, and leave to soak for 30 minutes in tepid water with I tsp salt. Drain and leave to dry.

Melt the butter in a saucepan, add the rice and stir until the grains are coated with butter. Pour in the hot stock so that it comes about 5mm (¼in) above the level of the rice. Use a piece of dampened baking parchment to cover the rice, put on the lid and cook on a medium heat for 5 minutes.

Lower to a very slow simmer for another 5 minutes, or until little holes start to appear in the surface and all of the liquid has been absorbed.

Tip the rice into a large bowl and mix in the spices, together with the quartered stuffed olives and the chopped coriander.

Preheat the oven to 220°C/gas mark 7.

Stuff the chickens with some of the rice mixture. Put a few spoonfuls into an oiled roasting dish, just where the chickens will sit. Make the piles quite high so there's plenty for the lovely chicken juices to sink into. Set the remaining rice aside for later. Cook until crispy and tender: about 1½ hours.

When the chickens are cooked, remove from the pan and add the rice from the baking tray to the boiled rice you've set aside.

Give it a good stir so that the juicy rice from the tin mixes well into the other spicy rice.

Joint the chickens. Pile the rice on to a serving dish and lay the chicken pieces on top. Garnish with fried almonds.

Dina and Dad at a family party – not a wake!

My Mum: A French Huguenot in Croydon

A couple of years ago my sister Julia took part in the BBC programme *Who Do You Think You Are?* and since then a fair few people have come up to one or other of us saying things like, 'Wow, how fascinating that your father was a member of an actual Bedouin tribe!'

Julia and I always reply very politely, making all the right noises but in actual fact secretly thinking, 'Yes, the Arabic story is fascinating, but the fact that we found out that our mum's ancestors were French Huguenots was far more fascinating to us!' Bless my mother. Rightly or wrongly, Dad's heritage always takes centre stage, whilst Mum's always waits in the wings. Well, let's redress the balance a little.

The programme followed our mother's roots back to the somewhat persecuted French Huguenots and discovered that, in all probability, her direct ancestors were lacemakers and dress designers, traditional Huguenot professions. There's a touching moment in the programme when Mum and Julia visit a Huguenot graveyard in the knowledge that distant relatives were more than likely buried there. It was very emotional for Mum, as not only her love of things French but also her passion for fine textiles and antique materials took on a more substantial meaning. In many regards, suddenly 'things made a lot more sense'.

You see, all through our childhood we knew that our mother's interest in, or rather her obsession with, all things French wasn't simply that of a keen Francophile. For a long time we've been convinced that other forces must be at play — forces much stronger than just the lure of cheap plonk in Calais! Given any opportunity, Mum would enthuse about France and all things French. In a breath she'd jump from how beautiful the country, the weather, the food, the language were to how infectious the bohemian café lifestyle was and how wonderful the art galleries were. Her heart and mind were so firmly in *la belle France* that my sisters and I sometimes feared that one day she might head over there and never return!

Any excuse she could find (like something as run of the mill as,

'We've run out of olive oil' — no joke) and, before you could say '*tout le monde*', she was halfway to Dover, clutching a cut-price ferry ticket and joyfully '*au revoir-ing*' us all.

Of course, being the conscientious wife and mother she was, she'd always come back the same day (albeit on the very last ferry possible), laden with shopping.

Opening the boot of the car was like peering into a treasure chest: a huge selection of great big smelly cheeses, always eliciting a chorus of 'ooooeeerrrr', followed by feigned passings-out and accusations of having smelly feet; enormous paper bags of croissants, already en route to staleness and therefore in desperate need of our immediate care and attention in the form of some butter and strawberry confiture; a ludicrous number of bottles and boxes of bargain-basement booze, with all their fabulously foreign labels; and one of our real delights, those strange-tasting, fancy French biscuits, which (simply because they'd been bought in Calais) were the only shop-bought biscuits we were ever allowed to eat as kids.

Rather alarmingly, somewhere in the dark depths of her boot there would always be, lurking with intent, a whole skinned rabbit, which would cause my father's eyes to light up and our stomachs to turn. More often than not there would also be a *très, très* foreign-looking, dark, fleshy hen (dead, of course), which meant my mum's delicious coq au vin was definitely going to be on that week's menu — hoorah!

And so, with the car emptied, the living room and kitchen a scene of Gallic gastronomic chaos, with the obligatory French onions rolling everywhere, we'd all dive back into the bags to re-survey the booty. It was now that we'd discover those little added extras that Mum had ferreted into the bottom of a bag: an unusual type of mushroom, a rarely seen cheese, a weird cut of meat or, on one particular occasion, a strange, triangular-shaped thing in a shiny box. 'What's this?' I asked.

'What do you mean?' Mum replied, shattered from her journey and already on the Beaujolais. 'Oh that! Well, it's a nasal blackhead steamer, of course.' My face screwed up with horror. 'Aren't the French bloody brilliant?' she said, draining her first glass.

So there you have it: my mum — a Huguenot in Croydon!

A Poor Man's Coq au Vin

We go to town with birthday gatherings in our family. For Mum's seventieth, my sisters and I transformed our conservatory (it's actually more of a lean-to) into a fabulously French bistro. We had red-and-white chequered tablecloths, French flags and buckets full of baguettes; false moustaches for the boys (of course), berets for the girls, and Edith Piaf singing her heart out ('a cat going through a mincer', according to Mark).

It was a great night, made even better by the delicious retro bistro menu. Dina created the most wonderfully over-the-top prawn cocktails, which literally brought gasps from the guests as we paraded them out. I made Mum's coq au vin, sticking to the letter of her recipe, and an obscene mountain of profiteroles, which Julia covered in *très* elegant candles. It was such a special night and hopefully Mum felt very loved and, more importantly, very well fed!

P.S. Surprise, surprise, my herby garlic bread (see page 62) goes really well with this.

SERVES 4

1 medium chicken, jointed
vegetable oil
1 bottle fruity red wine
a good handful bacon pieces
1 medium onion, peeled and sliced
2 large garlic cloves, peeled and crushed
2 heaped tsp tomato purée
2 sprigs fresh thyme, or 2–3 good pinches dried thyme
1 bay leaf
salt and black pepper
900g (2lb) potatoes, peeled and cut into 5cm (2in) pieces,
    or *beurre manié* (made with 25g (1oz) each plain flour and
    softened butter)

For the garnish

12–18 button onions, or small shallots, peeled
25g (1oz) butter
125ml (4 fl. oz) dry Martini or Noilly Prat (or white wine
    if you prefer, but the Martini gives an extra herby hit)
1 dsp Marigold vegetable bouillon
225g (8oz) small button mushrooms
2 tbsp finely chopped fresh parsley

Fry the chicken pieces in a little oil until golden, then put into a large bowl and pour the wine over. Leave to marinate overnight.

In a large stewing pot, fry the bacon pieces in a little more oil, then add the onion and garlic. When the onion is translucent, add the tomato purée and fry for a couple of minutes more. Add the chicken (except for the breasts) and wine to the pot, then the herbs and seasoning. Bring to the boil, then simmer or, better still, cook in a medium oven (180°C/gas mark 4) for about 30 minutes, until the chicken is almost cooked, adding the potatoes (if using) after the first 15 minutes. Then add the breasts, return to the heat and cook for about another 15 minutes, or until the chicken is all cooked through. If you're not adding potatoes to the pot, use *beurre manié* to thicken the sauce at the end of the cooking.

Meanwhile, for the garnish, fry the onions in half the butter and a little oil over a medium heat in a heavy pan, shaking the pan so that they roll and get evenly browned, for about 10 minutes. When they're golden, splash in the Martini and the vegetable bouillon, and leave to simmer for another 8–10 minutes, until the onions are tender.

Put the remaining butter and a little oil in a frying pan and, once the butter has stopped foaming, throw in the whole mushrooms and fry briskly, tossing them around for 4–5 minutes. Don't overcrowd the pan or they won't brown but will just give out lots of liquid and steam. Once they have browned, remove from the heat. This can be done ahead of time and then the mushrooms and onions can be reheated.

Arrange the chicken pieces and potatoes on a serving dish, pour the luscious sauce all over the top, and garnish with those lovingly prepared onions and mushrooms, and the parsley. *Bon appétit, mes petits pois!*

Mademoiselle Julia at Mum's seventieth birthday party when we brought France to South London. What a party!

Up the Duff and Married in Just Eight Months

Both my husband Mark and I are Scorpions. Not literally, obviously, but astrologically. Which is shorthand for saying we're pretty impulsive in *every* way. So it came as no surprise that within just eight months of meeting each other we found ourselves standing at the end of the aisle in Dulwich College Chapel saying, 'I do', with me three months pregnant. Yep. In every department we moved fast.

It was an 'unusual' ceremony. I had secretly arranged for everyone to have a small bag, in which there was a miniature of vodka to swig from, a packet of love-message sweets and (timed to coincide with when I wheeled Mark round to face the crowd), a pair of rose-tinted glasses for each of them to wear as I shared *my* vows. This, coupled with the fact that I announced my 'up-the-duffness' for the first time to most friends and family members whilst at the altar, and then had 'Dancing Queen' (Abba, of course) playing as we walked out, meant poor old Mark didn't really know what had hit him. (In fact, I don't think he really knew who I *was*, his stag night having been only two nights before!)

Thankfully, 2 June 2001 was a beautifully sunny day amongst weeks of rain. Once the marriage ceremony had finished, we all piled back to my mum and dad's garden, where a huge marquee had been erected and beautifully decorated by friends and family. As our 150 guests slowly arrived to celebrate the two lunatics getting hitched, we had to do that 'thing' they do at weddings, when the bride and groom welcome every guest. Well, we started off with the best of intentions, but quite quickly the sheer volume of faces bedazzled us both. I distinctly remember Mark covertly jotting down the names of my various relatives into a small notebook (Nael, Nayef, Nabi, Nabil, Leila, Ingrid, Laurice, Elias, Mazin and Jamileh) and alongside them he would write their relationship to me. To this day he curses having lost that notebook …

We had a cornucopia of all my favourite Arabic dishes: Uncle

Nabil's magnificent whole spiced lamb, my mum's rebel vine leaves, my 'fantastic' falafels, Auntie Jamileh's (corrected) sfeeha, Auntie Ilham's spicy kofta served with bowls of cool mint yogurt, trays of my Palestinian mussakhan, a huge dish of mansaf (of course, as 'you can't have a wedding without a mansaf') and pots of real family favourites like roz-bil-hummus and sheikh-al-mahshi. The list went on and on but, believe it or not, Mark didn't manage to have a single mouthful of anything. Not because there wasn't enough; it was a more a case of it being so divine everyone ate far too quickly. In fact, the evening instalment of food disappeared within 20 minutes! It was one of those rare culinary occasions when vegetarians lapsed for 24 hours, meat-eaters dabbled in the unspeakable joys of vegan food and, well, everyone just royally scoffed their hearts out, with the sole exception of the bride and groom.

For our wedding cake we had a beautiful (ahead of its time) fairy-cakes fountain, with two little director's chairs perched on the top, one that read DIRECTOR on its back, the other PRESENTER. The irony, as Mark said in his speech, is that if ever there was a presenter who tended to direct everything and everyone in her path, it was me, whilst Mark, in turn, would give any melodramatic actress a good run for her money!

All was going great until about 8 p.m. when our hardcore friends started to arrive, and within a matter of minutes a twinkling, fairy-like haven of marital celebration had transformed into a bit of a circus. One friend was such a comedy drunk he kept saying 'I am jusht sho sho sho happy for them. Sho happy I could cry', then promptly fell backwards through the marquee's awning on top of a couple hiding from the crowds. Quite suddenly, and violently, a very camp friend of Mark's appeared to be fired from an enormous catapult, mowing down every single imported exotic plant, flower display and relative en route, in his urgency to hug and congratulate my husband. Mark's mate John passed out in our wheelbarrow and was christened Wheelbarrow Man by the kids. We had bouncers on the door to prevent the arrival of one of Mark's ex-girlfriends and someone's 'uncle' tried to woo another one of Mark's exes (there were a lot of

Mark's exes at our wedding). A certain crowd transformed the potting shed into a den of iniquity (the less said about that the better); a cameraman friend of ours met a production co-coordinator friend of ours and they have since got engaged; a car was driven into the front wall of my parents' house; a very athletic geriatric went flying off the dance floor; someone had some sort of seizure; someone else lost their dentures (which, interestingly, were found three months later, somewhat strangely and ghoulishly clenched around a pair of Mark's Ray-Ban sunglasses which were also lost on the day) … and so it went on until the following morning.

When we got up to leave for the airport and our honeymoon on the Amalfi Coast, in the flowerbed on the opposite side of the road we could see the soles of various people's shoes — people who had literally crashed there and then, rather than heading home. As they emerged, groggy and bleary-eyed, not one of them (nor any other guest at our wedding) could remember a single thing apart from the fact that 'the food was bloody good'.

Mark tucking in!

Sheikh-al-Mahshi *(The King of All Stuffed Vegetables)*

This is known throughout the Arab world as 'the king of stuffed ones'.

SERVES 2–4
4 small aubergines
4 green peppers
olive oil
1 large onion, peeled and finely minced
1 large garlic clove, peeled and finely chopped
2 tbsp pine nuts
900g (2lb) minced lamb (not too finely minced)
2 tsp baharat spice mix (see page 120), or ground allspice
a bunch fresh parsley, chopped
salt and black pepper
2 tbsp tomato purée
600ml (1 pint) water (or enough to cover the vegetables)

Preheat the oven to 190°C/gas mark 5.

Remove the leaves and make a slit down one side of the aubergines from top to bottom. (If the aubergine is curved, make the slit on the inward-curving side.) Scoop out most of the flesh, leaving a shell of about 5mm (¼ in) all the way round. Discard the flesh.

Cut round the tops of the peppers, leaving about 2.5cm (1in) uncut, so that you can re-attach it. Scoop out the seeds.

Fry the aubergine shells and peppers in some oil in a large pan until they just begin to brown. Remove from the pan.

Add a little more oil to the pan and fry the onion and garlic until they're soft. Remove from the pan, then fry the pine nuts. Remove these from the pan, then fry the lamb and the spice until it just begins to brown. Right at the end, throw in a big handful of the parsley and stir. Throw the onions and pine nuts back into the pan and add salt and plenty of black pepper.

Stuff the aubergines and peppers with this mixture. Stuff them full, but don't press down too hard. Close the lids on the peppers. Arrange the aubergines and peppers close together in the bottom of a shallow ovenproof dish.

Mix the tomato purée, seasoned with salt and pepper, with just enough water to cover the vegetables. Pour this mixture over the vegetables and bake until the aubergines and peppers are tender: about 30 minutes. The sauce should have reduced halfway down. Sprinkle with the rest of the chopped parsley and enjoy!

Desert Island Dishes

Four years ago my husband and I took a semi-suicidal leap into the world of TV production. It was something Mark had wanted to do for some time, and I cannot even begin to describe how difficult and competitive it is to set up and run your own TV production company.

The irony was that, relatively quickly, we got our first commission for the BBC. The double irony was that it was Mark (a documentary maker and self-confessed non-foodie) who got it: making a food programme with my culinary hero, Nigel Slater.

Called *A Taste of My Life*, the show was inspired by two things: first, Nigel Slater's book *Toast*, and second, one of our favourite radio shows, *Desert Island Discs*. In the end it ran for four series and featured the lives of over thirty very bloody famous people!

Throughout this time our home became a very strange place. As Mark and his team booked guests and filmed the shows, every now and then I would (as food producer) have to troubleshoot last-minute requests from guests. It was quite normal to overhear stressed exchanges along the lines of: 'So what's the story behind Vanessa Redgrave's banana, chocolate and mince stew?' (I am not kidding); 'Get Simon Schama's venison stew in a cab for Nigella Lawson — now!'; 'OK!' I scream from the kitchen, and 'What do you mean John Hurt's suckling pig has done a runner …?'

Well, in the final series one of our guests was the lovely actor Denis Lawson. The day before we were due to film with Denis at the studio, Mark went out to get a quick interview with his best mate, the actor John Gordon Sinclair. The interview supplied the show with 'A Tasty Challenge' — a dish that Denis and Nigel would have to cook with no preparation time, just the ingredients and a never-before-seen recipe. This is where yours truly stepped in.

Mark came back with his hysterical interview and I discovered that the challenge of the day was to be a Moroccan pigeon b'stilla. Whilst most of the film crew winced at the thought of pigeons in a pie and got an early night, I burned the midnight oil fine-tuning the b'stilla recipe that I hoped would wow not only Denis Lawson, but (fear of fears) Nigel Slater as well. Guess what … they both loved it. Phew!

A Taste of Morocco (Pigeon Pie)

I must admit this classic Moroccan dish is a very fancy and time-consuming one but, believe me, it is also very delicious. I learned how to make it from a fabulous cook and family friend, Fatima, and we always knew how close to her heart we were, because whenever we visited her home this is what we were lovingly served.

So, if you want to spoil someone special to you, *this* is the recipe to go for. Oh, it's also a great dish if you want to induce jealousy in someone who deserves it!

P.S. Don't stint on the butter. I made that mistake when I cooked this dish for Simon Rimmer on *Eating in the Sun* — he said it was very dry. He was not a happy bunny, as he had flown all the way to Marrakech to eat. *Sooooo* embarrassing ...

SERVES 6
15 sheets ready-made filo pastry
110g (4oz) butter, melted
1 free-range egg yolk, beaten
For the filling
90g (3¼oz) butter
2 onions, peeled and grated
8 pigeons, gutted and cleaned, or 4 poussins, halved
1–2 tsp fine salt
1 tsp freshly ground black pepper
3 tbsp chopped fresh parsley
3 tbsp chopped fresh coriander
½ tsp saffron powder, infused in a little boiling water
1 tsp ground cinnamon
55g (2oz) caster sugar
600ml (1 pint) chicken stock
3 tbsp vegetable oil
280g (10oz) blanched almonds
7 free-range egg yolks, beaten
To serve
3–4 tbsp icing sugar
1 tbsp ground cinnamon

For the filling, melt the butter in a large pan over a medium heat. Add the onion and stir over a low heat for 5–6 minutes. Add the pigeons and cook for 10 minutes, turning occasionally. Add the salt and pepper, the parsley, coriander, saffron (already in its water), cinnamon and half the sugar, and stir well. Add the stock and bring to the boil. Reduce the heat to a simmer, cover with a lid and cook over a low heat for 30 minutes, or until the pigeons are cooked and tender, stirring from time to time and adding a little water if necessary. Remove the pigeons from the pan and allow them to cool. Remove the pigeon meat from the bones and shred coarsely.

Meanwhile heat the oil in a small pan, add the almonds and fry, stirring constantly until golden brown. Remove the almonds with a slotted spoon and drain for a few minutes on kitchen paper. Crush the almonds coarsely in a mortar, or chop in a grinder for a very short time (we don't want them turning to a paste). Put the crushed almonds into a bowl with the remaining sugar and 2 tbsp of the oil from the pan.

Return the pan in which the birds were cooked to the heat and simmer the cooking liquid for 10–15 minutes, stirring constantly, until it has reduced by three-quarters. Turn the heat to very low and add the egg yolk to the reduced liquid. Cook over a low heat, stirring all the time until the sauce thickens enough to coat a spoon.

Preheat the oven to 180°C/gas mark 4.

Time to put the pie together! Oil a 30cm (12in) round baking tin. (Remember that once the filo pastry is out of the packet, you must keep it under a damp tea-towel to prevent it from drying out.) Layer five sheets of filo pastry into the tin, brushing each one with plenty of melted butter and laying them at angles across each other, fanning them round the tin so that about 10cm (4in) of each filo sheet hangs over the edge of the tin. Then add two more sheets across the base, buttering each as you add it. Trim any edges that are too big for the tin.

Cover the base with the egg mixture, then lay two more sheets of pastry over it. Brush with melted butter and trim off any excess around the edges.

Spread the shredded pigeon meat over the pastry, then top with another two layers of buttered filo pastry. Sprinkle the almond mixture over the top and cover with the remaining filo, buttering each sheet before adding the next layer. Fold any excess pastry over the top to cover the pie, gently pushing the sheets down. When the pie is cooked, the sheets will curl upwards a bit.

Brush the top of the pie with, you've guessed it, more melted butter, then brush with beaten egg yolk all over. Pop into the preheated oven and bake for 40 minutes, or until golden brown and crisp.

To serve, turn out the pie on to a large dish. For a traditional flourish, sprinkle with icing sugar and cinnamon in a lattice-like pattern.

Simon Rimmer's Moroccan Dinner

Sticking with the Moroccan theme, the last show we shot in our series *Eating in the Sun* was an episode in Marrakech. Mark, our four girls and I adore Morocco, and for this shoot we decided to combine a holiday for the girls and Nanny Di (Mark's mother) with our work trip. Memories of this culinary adventure will, I think, stay with all of us for a very long time. This was one of those jobs that make you feel very grateful for the work you do.

We went crocus-picking in the foothills of the Atlas mountains for saffron, we visited a women's refuge where they hand-manufacture a most divine product called argan oil, and we went to a Berber settlement and learned how to make traditional couscous before eating it under a tent in the desert. The girls came with us on all these journeys and were smitten with everything they saw and everything they tasted. I remember re-living a small part of my own childhood whenever I looked off camera to see all those little wide-eyed faces staring back at me as I 'performed' in front of camera. How things had changed from my father fighting imaginary mythical monsters in the nearby deserts as a young actor, to me now presenting my own food series. As you can imagine, Morocco is a very special and magical place for all of us.

This idyll, however, was shortlived. Having learned (with great difficulty) to cook a four-course spread of Moroccan food, this North African paradise was somewhat wrecked by the sudden arrival of the final mystery chef in the series – none other than tough nut and TV chef Simon Rimmer.

All I can diplomatically say is that I didn't exactly excel at some of the dishes I cooked up for him. Whether it was bad luck, or simply that I was exhausted having reached the end of the series, every single nightmare that could have happened happened. I won't re-embarrass myself by listing all my kitchen disasters (after all, they'll be in the BBC vaults for eternity now), but suffice it to say that one of the regional dishes, called tangia (a one-pot lamb stew cooked in a nearby baker's oven dug into the ground and used by the entire neighbourhood), was going very well until I realized we had accidentally picked up the wrong tangia pot at the baker's and had nearly served Simon a dish cooked by the woman who lived at number 37.

Well, the recipe I'm offering up to you from this experience is something I didn't actually cook for the programme but have begun to cook regularly at home. Having fallen flat on our faces, we had the wrap-party dinner at a nearby riad (a traditional Moroccan house or palace built around a garden) and — with all our daughters in tow, spending the entire night trying to pull increasingly ridiculous faces (see photos) — we ate a fabulous local dish that is now a favourite for all of us. I cannot even begin to tell you the relief I felt, knowing that I no longer suddenly had to jump up and serve this dish to some pesky celebrity chef. No, with this dish I simply sat back and spent the night laughing and eating these divine spicy meatballs with my lovely family — pulling ludicrous faces.

Manic Mask

Frazzled Fleur

Ill Issy

Mad Maddie

Me after twelve vodkas

Spicy Moroccan Meatballs, Egg and Chips

In Moroccan kitchens they don't fry the spices or onions, but that just goes against every fibre of my culinary being, so I apologize if I cause offence to anyone with this recipe. It is my favourite Moroccan treat, so please try it. It's also deeply satisfying to make as well as to eat.

SERVES 4-6

For the meatballs
1kg (2¼lb) minced lamb
1 large onion, peeled and finely grated
4 tsp each ground cumin and ground coriander
2 tsp each paprika, ground ginger and ground cinnamon
½ large bunch fresh coriander, finely chopped
½ large bunch fresh parsley, finely chopped

For the sauce
3-4 tbsp olive oil
1 large onion, peeled and finely chopped
2 tsp each ground cumin, ground coriander and paprika
½ tsp cayenne pepper
2 tbsp tomato purée
2 x 400g (14oz) cans chopped tomatoes
2 tbsp each chopped fresh parsley and coriander
a pinch granulated sugar
1 egg per person

Put the ingredients for the meatballs into a mixing bowl and mix until almost a paste. In Morocco the women wet their hands before shaping the mixture into walnut-sized balls. Once rolled, pop them in the fridge to firm up.

For the sauce, put the oil into a tagine (or a deep, heavy-based frying pan) and fry the onion really slowly until it's gloopy. Now sprinkle in all the spices and stir until the aroma is released.

Add the tomato purée and fry until the colour changes, then add the tomatoes, parsley, coriander and sugar. Bring up to a near boil, then simmer very slowly for 15 minutes. Add a little water if the sauce looks a bit thick.

You can now drop in your spicy meatballs and simmer for 30 minutes. Don't fiddle about with them or you'll end up with broken balls – ouch!

With a spoon, make little hollows in the sauce and carefully crack in the eggs. Cover and simmer gently until the eggs are cooked to your liking: 5–10 minutes.

In Morocco this dish is taken to the table and everyone dips in with freshly baked baguettes. They often serve French fries with it too, which is really, really good, and always causes gasps of appreciation whenever I serve them.

Return to the Holy Lamb

As a child I witnessed, on more than one occasion, various grown men from my family weeping over a lamb dish that in one way or another was not *exactly* as it should be.

You see, any self-respecting Arab insists that lamb should be cooked to the point of such tenderness that it is best eaten with a spoon. They also need it to be packed with plenty of garlic, spices and (in my family) slivers of fresh ginger. Most Arabs also insist on their lamb being accompanied with butter-fried almond rice and a huge pot of vegetables stewed to within an inch of their lives.

The consequences of growing up around such fanatical and exacting standards is that the thought of creating my own lamb recipe has literally filled me with such a fear of failure for years now that I've simply stuck with the tried and tested recipes that were handed down to my aunties, cousins and grandparents from as far back as when Moses parted the Red Sea.

Then, out of the blue, almost a year ago I woke up in a cold sweat. As I came to, fumbling for the bedside light, I could have sworn I heard the sound of the archangels singing. It dawned on me that today, *now* I had to break with tradition. Today was the day I would have the courage to create my very own lamb recipe.

Taking care not to wake my husband, I tiptoed downstairs to the kitchen. As my pulse rate increased I opened my fridge and slowly but certainly took out my freshly bought leg of lamb.

I was about to go against hundreds of years of tradition. In my own way, I was about to enter culinary history, risking the fury of my tribe. 'By the end of this recipe,' I thought, 'there's a very good chance that, if I'm not careful, and if my Auntie Jamileh finds out, I'll be the lamb that's taken to the slaughter ...' So this had better be good, this had better be bloody good!

The leg of lamb was a beautiful piece of organic meat from my local butcher's, so I knew it would have great flavour. I wanted to enhance this rather than mask it, so I decided I'd roast it until just perfectly pink with sweet, sticky roasted garlic and plenty of seasoning. I can almost hear the horrified screams of my Arab ancestors!

The 'I-did-it-my-way' Leg of Lamb

Mark adores mint sauce (making his own, with his ludicrously vast selection of mints from the herb garden) and he also loves pesto, so I thought I'd have a bit of a play with these flavours. I swapped the basil for mint and the pine nuts for pistachios, adding a splash of Spanish sherry vinegar to give the whole thing a little kick. He loved it, and had it all over his vegetables as well as his lamb.

SERVES 6

2.7kg (6lb) leg of lamb
4 whole garlic bulbs, with skins on, plus 2 extra cloves,
   peeled and finely sliced
olive oil
coarse sea salt
freshly ground black pepper
For the parsley and mint pesto
6 tbsp fresh mint leaves
6 tbsp fresh parsley leaves
2 garlic cloves
300g (10oz) chopped pistachio nuts
225ml (8 fl. oz) olive oil
a splash Spanish sherry vinegar

Take the lamb out of the fridge an hour or so before you cook it. Preheat the oven to 220°C/gas mark 7.

Slice the garlic bulbs horizontally in two and lay them in a roasting tin. Drizzle olive oil over them and sprinkle with sea salt.

Now rub the lamb with oil and rub in plenty of sea salt and cracked black pepper. Insert some slivers of the sliced garlic into the meat. Place the joint on top of the cut heads of garlic and pop into the oven for 15 minutes, just to get it sizzling. I find this really helps to give it a nice, crispy brown skin.

Turn the oven down to 180°C/gas mark 4 and cook for another 15 minutes per 450g (1lb): roughly another 1½ hours. Remove from the oven and leave to rest, loosely covered, for a minimum of 15 minutes.

While the lamb is cooking you can make the pesto. Process the mint, parsley and garlic in a blender until they're very finely chopped, then add the nuts, at the same time pouring in the olive oil very slowly, until everything is blended. Stir in the vinegar, season well and pour into a small jug.

Carve the lamb and serve with the sauce.

A World of Make-believe

If I had any sense I wouldn't tell you about my elder sister Dina, as she's such a good cook you might start lusting after a book written by *her* rather than *me*.

There's two years between us and as little girls we were incredibly close — so close in fact that aged just six and eight we got married and had babies! We called this game of domestic bliss — where, strangely, *both* our names were Salah — 'The Salahs' (don't ask us *why*). We also had our own car (two old bright orange milk crates, with a suction toy steering wheel and wooden-spoon gearstick), our own detached house with garden (a manky old fleece blanket draped over an old wooden clothes horse with a rubber plant firmly placed just outside) and, best of all, we had our very own Salah language. For example 'Wa la momo lapana?', loosely translated, meant 'What's for dinner, darling?', and believe me we said these words often, as cooking played a huge part in our complex game.

We used to spend hours making pretend gourmet food and one of our favourite creations was lemon meringue pie. We would start by making a delicately light pastry with some stolen flour and the very finest orange squash. Then we'd whip up the perfect creamy lemon filling using yellow toilet paper and ludicrously expensive, stolen face-cream. Then, being the little geniuses we were, we'd make the most exquisite meringue topping with bars of Imperial Leather soap, which we would wet and rub frantically between our hands until we had enough bubbles to spread all over the lemon filling. Later we progressed to stolen shaving cream, which was a great time-saver.

From the look on Dina's face, she's jealous of my pants.

As we grew up, we continued with our cooking *and* our evaluating of each other's food, and as a teenager Dina excelled in whatever cuisine she experimented with, usually determined by the nationality of whatever boyfriend she had at the time.

My personal favourite, however, was her Italian phase. Oh boy, she loved Italy: the art, the architecture and the men, and, luckily for the rest of the family, she adored the food. Yes, thanks to Massimo, or was it Stefano (actually, come to think of it, it might have been Ricardo) — well, whatever his *name* was, the upshot was that we were treated to some of the very best that Italian cuisine had to offer.

Dina's passion for all things Italian was so intense, she actually believed that if she cooked like an Italian mama she would become Italian. So, as well as learning how to speak fluent Italian, she also worked tirelessly on perfecting all those iconic Italian dishes like polenta with spicy sausage, perfectly thin pizzas made with the finest buffalo mozzarella and her grown-in-her-own-bedroom basil, creamy risottos and utterly delicious pasta dishes using strange ingredients like squid ink and broccoli. Then there was *my* personal favourite: pollo sorpresa, or 'chicken surprise' to you and me, the 'surprise' being the gorgeous garlic-herb butter that would ooze out of a perfectly breaded and fried chicken breast, finished off with a sprinkle of parsley and a not-to-be-forgotten squeeze of lemon. Simply mouthwatering ...

In actual fact I hardly ever make this dish for myself, always living in the vain hope that my lovely, gorgeous, generous, clever, witty ... (hope you're reading, Dina) ... beautiful, skilful, talented ... (you'd better skip to the recipe, I'm going to be some time here convincing her to come over and make this for me, even though it's not my birthday) — where was I ? ... oh, yes ... funny, kind, slim, knowledgeable, instinctive ... please, please, please ...

Pollo Sorpresa (*Chicken Surprise*)

On the rare occasions I make this myself, I love to have a green salad with a lemon and olive oil dressing and some plain boiled potatoes or rice to 'mush' into the butter.

SERVES 4
4 boneless chicken breasts, skinned
juice of 1 lemon
55g (2oz) plain flour
salt and black pepper
115g (4oz) very fine stale breadcrumbs
1 egg white, beaten
sunflower oil
For the butter stuffing
115g (4oz) salted butter, softened
2 tbsp chopped fresh parsley
1 tbsp dried oregano
3 garlic cloves, peeled and chopped
To serve
2 tbsp chopped fresh parsley
1 lemon, quartered

For the butter stuffing, mix the butter, herbs and garlic, season with salt and pepper, then pop it into the freezer whilst you prepare the chicken.

Preheat the oven to 180°C/gas mark 4.

Lay a piece of cling film down, then put the chicken breasts on it. Lay another piece of cling film on top and bash with a rolling pin until the breasts are flattened but not too thin. Rub some lemon juice over each breast and season.

Get three flat bowls and put the flour, seasoned with salt and pepper, in one and the breadcrumbs and egg white in the other two. Divide the garlic butter into four equal amounts and put each one on to the end of each of the four chicken breasts. Roll the breasts up, folding in the sides (if they're misbehaving, you can fix them with cocktail sticks). Roll them in the seasoned flour, then the egg white and finally the breadcrumbs, making sure every part of the meat is covered. Pop them in the fridge for 20 minutes to firm them up.

In a heavy-bottomed frying pan, slowly heat the oil until it's hot enough to sizzle round a piece of bread. Gently lower the chicken into the pan and fry until light golden brown all over. Pop into the oven for 20–30 minutes until cooked through.

Serve with a sprinkle of parsley and a squeeze of lemon juice.

A Slightly Tipsy Tepsi

Tepsi is a very popular and *very* delicious Iraqi dish that uses aubergines, potatoes, onions, tomatoes, garlic and spices, all of which are fried first and then layered and baked in the oven. It's a fabulous dish if you have both vegetarians and meat-lovers in your midst, as it can be either a meal in its own right or a fabulous accompaniment to roast lamb, or indeed, as our Iraqi plumber once stated (just at the point he was about to unblock the u-bend), 'It is craziness not to try it with chicken.'

I learned how to make it from my mum's friend Liz (a lovely but utterly barmy Scotswoman), who was married to an even barmier Iraqi man. She always used to make it when she was escaping the stifling Iraqi summer heat, taking a mini-vacation at our house in Streatham.

Apparently, as a child I always pronounced it 'tipsy' instead of 'tepsi', at which all the adults would fall about laughing. Like many mispronunciations within my family, it has stuck and no one (including my kids) would dream of calling tepsi anything other than tipsy. Confused? Try cooking it when you're tipsy and you certainly will be, as it's a 'wee bit fiddly' to quote Liz. In fact, she used to say this constantly whilst cooking it, prompting my mother to laugh uproariously every time. I realize in retrospect why I might have always called it 'tipsy'!

But she was right: it *is* a 'wee bit fiddly', as everything is fried separately. But it's a lovely dish to choose when you fancy spending a bit more time in the kitchen. You know the sort of thing: in the house on your own … music on … a nice glass of wine … slowly getting tepsi cooking tipsy …

Tepsi (Aubergine, Onion and Potato Bake)

This dish fills the house with such a delicious aroma that guests are instantly soothed the moment you open your front door.

SERVES 4
2 aubergines, thickly sliced
salt and black pepper
2 large potatoes, peeled
2 large tomatoes
2 large onions, peeled
4 garlic cloves, peeled
olive oil
vegetable oil
2–3 tsp ground mixed spice
200ml (7 fl. oz) lamb or veg stock
juice of ½ lemon
1 tbsp tomato purée

Me and Mark, blissed out on our honeymoon in Ischia (we've never been on our own since!).

Preheat the oven to 180°C/gas mark 4.

Put the sliced aubergines into a colander, then sprinkle salt all over them and leave them like this for about an hour. It won't be the end of the world if you don't have time to do this bit, but it does sort out a couple of things. First, it draws out the bitterness that can sometimes be present in aubergines, and it also means less oil is absorbed at the frying stage.

Now slice the potatoes, tomatoes and onions to the same thickness as the aubergines, and thinly slice the garlic.

Pour 2–3 glugs olive oil (maybe more) into a frying pan and gently fry the onions and garlic until they just start to turn brown, then remove with a slotted spoon. Add a splash of vegetable oil to the olive oil and bring slowly up to heat. Put the potatoes in and fry nice and slowly until golden brown and almost cooked through, then remove and set aside. Rinse the salt off the aubergines and dry thoroughly with kitchen paper. Again, add a bit more oil and bring up to heat (very important: if your oil is not hot enough you'll get very greasy aubergines), then gently fry the aubergine until golden brown. Remove and put on kitchen paper to absorb excess oil.

I use a ceramic pie dish to alternate layers of onion, potato, tomato and aubergine, sprinkling the mixed spices, salt and pepper throughout this process. I then pour the stock, lemon juice and tomato purée into the dish and bake, uncovered, for 50–60 minutes.

The Food of Love . . .

Picking Up the Presenter

The story behind Mark and me getting together is a funny one. It took a strange detour to Bristol for us to meet, even though (we later discovered) we'd both lived on the same street for several years. Perhaps funniest of all, we met on a dating show called *Perfect Partners* and after over twenty episodes featuring over forty dates, the only coupling that happened in the entire series was between Mark and me. We literally found each other's 'perfect partner' and it was a mad and magical time.

Stranger still, the first night we kissed was on location in glorious Blackpool. Not the place either of us imagined meeting lifelong partners. Even funnier, Mark has kept the 'call sheet' (the listed itinerary issued to all members of the film crew) for this shoot — and it makes us roar with laughter because it says '17.00 PICK UP PRESENTER'. What this means on a call sheet is, quite literally, 'go to the station and pick up the presenter'. As Pete, our boss in Bristol, pointed out, perhaps Mark misinterpreted the instructions.

Once 'picked up', a lot of that night was a passionate blur, but one lasting memory we *do* still have is of us both ordering five rounds of egg and cress sandwiches. Although one thing led to another, absolutely nothing led either of us to the egg and cress sandwiches.

It's funny to think that back then we regularly smoked and drank ourselves to within an inch of our lives (incidentally, always ordering egg and cress sandwiches as a midnight gesture towards 'good' behaviour). But, wow, how things have changed! Now Mark doesn't drink, neither of us smokes, we're both training for the London Marathon and Mark grows his own cress (alongside every other vegetable imaginable) for our more 'mature' egg and cress sandwiches.

Rather amusingly, whenever he brings in a bowl of mustard cress from the greenhouse to add to my lovingly prepared egg mayonnaise, we never really know whether to eat the finished sandwiches or, for old times' sake, have a cuddle and simply forget all about them.

Fancy Egg Mayonnaise Sandwiches

You'll make more mayonnaise than you'll need for one sandwich, but you can keep any that's left over for about a week in the fridge. If you're like Mark and me, you'll probably end up ignoring this sandwich anyway.

MAKES 1 SANDWICH
2 hard-boiled eggs
a handful organic mustard cress
   (if your old man doesn't grow it for you)
2 slices good bread
For the mayonnaise
3 free-range egg yolks
2 tsp Dijon mustard
1 tbsp white wine vinegar
salt and white pepper
300ml (½ pint) olive or flavourless oil
   (you could use half and half)

For the mayonnaise, put the egg yolks, mustard, vinegar and some salt and pepper into a small bowl and give them a whisk. Put the oil into a jug and add it really slowly to the egg mixture (almost a drop at a time to begin with), whisking continuously until you've used all the oil. Add a little extra taste: I sometimes use a squeeze of lemon juice or a drop more vinegar.

Mash the hard-boiled eggs with a healthy dollop of the mayonnaise and mix it thoroughly. Pile on to one slice of the bread and then lay on as much mustard cress as you fancy. Put the other slice of bread on top, then head off up the wooden hill to Bedfordshire …

The Way to a Man's Heart ...

Imagine being married to me and not being 'that bothered about food', to quote my husband.

Well, this was the state of affairs between Mark and me when we were first married, and it was very annoying! When it came to every other pleasure life had to offer, he had a voracious appetite: art, music, literature and cinema. But when it came to food, no — an iron wall of resistance was all I found. He felt restaurants were a rip-off, genuinely believed organic food was a money-spinning conspiracy ('It's just the same food in different packaging') and passionately despised any food programmes (boy, how that was to change).

So, when I used to utter the fateful sentence, 'If you could have anything in the world for dinner tonight, my darling, what would it be?', imagine my frustration when he delivered this chirpy answer: 'White fish, vegetables and new potatoes would be lovely.'

Now how many husbands can boast of a wife who, when she asks this question, has the genuine intention of cooking whatever is his heart's desire? Not many, I can tell you. Well, he's been blissfully unaware (for eight years now) how close to being walloped with my rolling pin he's been every time he's muttered that exact same answer to my question: 'White fish, vegetables and new potatoes would be lovely.' (It's weird. Every time he says this, for him it's as though it's the first time he's ever thought of it!)

I have to confess that on occasion it has made me seriously re-evaluate our marriage. For me, his desired dish couldn't have been more uninteresting. So for years I've cooked him this meal a couple of times a month, and every time he finishes eating it, he says a big 'thank you' with a distant look in his eye. The look that says, 'That wasn't quite what I meant.'

Finally, after years of struggling to improve this somewhat limited dish, we paid his fabulously eccentric eighty-five-year-old Nanny Thelma a visit in Mudeford near Christchurch and, for the first time since I've known her, she proceeded to make Mark and me a meal. Actually, her exact words as she went off to cook it were, 'This is my

Markie's favourite!' His embarrassment was palpable – but so too was his excitement at having 'white fish, vegetables and new potatoes' done … properly! In fact I'd never seen him quite as excited about a meal before.

No sooner had the first mouthful of lightly floured and fried, freshly caught plaice entered my mouth, followed by a beautifully crisp and new potato, finished off by some politically incorrect, overcooked veggies, than I fully understood why he'd been so excited. It was absolutely delicious (in the way that only a nan's meal can be). I realized that for the past however many years, the reason my long-suffering husband had repeatedly asked for the same thing was because I never got close to what he actually wanted!

So, having had my own experience of Nanny Thelma's white fish, vegetables and new potatoes, it's proved a positive minefield getting it right. (My top tip is to pop down to Mudeford and ask Nanny Thelma herself for the recipe if you fancy it.)

Instead, I've invented a number of recipes (none of which has fish anywhere near it) to lure him to the kitchen table. I think I can safely say he loves them all, and maybe loves me even more for them. Well, he'd better, if he knows what's good for him!

THE OPERATION HAD BEEN A SUCCESS, THE HAPPY COUPLE
WERE JOINED PERMANTLY AT THE EARLOBE.

Our wedding invitation –
we asked people to write a caption
below and bring it along on the day.

Seriously Luvverly Chicken

This has become Mark's all-time favourite supper, lunch, snack or indeed breakfast (on one occasion) – that's how much he loves it. So how about that, Nanny Thelma?

SERVES 2

2 boneless chicken breasts
olive oil
a large pinch each chopped fresh thyme, oregano and sage
2 garlic cloves, peeled and sliced
plenty of salt and pepper
a large handful wild mushrooms
4–8 slices Parma ham, depending on size (you want to be
  able to wrap the breasts completely in them)
a knob butter
2–3 glugs medium sherry
150ml (¼ pint) cream
chopped fresh chives

Bat out the chicken breasts until fairly thin. Rub with oil, then roll in the herbs and garlic. Season with salt and pepper. Occasionally I have time to leave these to marinate. If you can, I would advise it, but if not, don't worry.

Fry the mushrooms in I tbsp oil in a frying pan until browned. Remove with a slotted spoon and set aside.

Now wrap the pieces of Parma ham around each chicken breast. If you like, you can secure these with rosemary or cocktail sticks, though I usually don't.

Add a knob of butter to the mushroom pan, add the chicken and fry gently for 5–8 minutes, depending on the size of the breasts. Do keep checking in order to avoid the dreaded dry-chicken syndrome. (Use a sharp knife to check they're cooked all the way through if you're not sure.) Remove them and set aside.

Add the sherry to the pan and simmer to burn off the alcohol. Add the cream, give it a stir, then throw the chicken back in together with the mushrooms and baste with the creamy loveliness for a minute or so.

Place on a serving dish and sprinkle with the chopped chives.

We usually have this with a crisp green salad and my sherry vinegar dressing.

Pork with a Sticky Onion and Madeira Sauce

If I'm honest, I had my mum in mind more than Mark when I dreamed up this dish (but don't tell him that!), though it *has* become a firm favourite of his too. Mum is crazy about onions in any way, shape or form: fried, boiled, baked or even as a lone ingredient in a sandwich, hence the abundance of them with this pork dish — another of her favourites.

SERVES 4
olive oil
25g (1oz) butter
3 large onions, peeled and thinly sliced
1 dsp plain flour
salt and black pepper
2 glugs Madeira or sherry (I use Madeira)
4 pork chops
a handful fresh sage leaves, shallow-fried

In a heavy frying pan, gently heat 2 glugs of the oil and the butter. Add the onions and cook really slowly. You want them to become brown and sticky, so it'll take about 20 minutes. You'll need to stir every now and again so you don't get those nasty burnt bits. Stir in the flour and keep stirring for a minute or so. Season well, then add the Madeira. Burn off the alcohol by raising the heat, then lower it and simmer for 5 minutes.

Meanwhile get your grill really hot and season the pork chops with salt and pepper (putting extra salt on the fat to crisp it up). Put the chops under the grill and seal on both sides, then reduce the heat a little and grill on both sides until cooked through. I'd love to tell you exactly how long this will take, but it really depends on the thickness of the pork. But please, please, keep checking, as it's so easy to dry them out.

When the chops are ready, put them on a warmed plate and spoon some of the onion mixture all over them. Garnish with fried sage leaves. Plain boiled potatoes go perfectly with this dish.

Mark's Cheeky Chops

This is such a simple recipe, but the taste is out of this world, the anchovies creating a deep, intensely savoury flavour (not fishy at all) and the lamb being dreamily tender.

SERVES 4
4 large lamb chump chops
a small jar anchovies in oil (I use the one with chillies)
2 plump garlic cloves, peeled
sea salt and black pepper

Let the chops come up to room temperature. Put the rest of the ingredients in the liquidizer and whizz to a smooth paste.

Smother the chops on both sides with the paste, then season with freshly ground pepper and crunchy salt. I always sprinkle extra salt on the fat so that it goes irresistibly crispy.

Get your grill as hot as it goes and slam the lamb under. Grill until the fat starts to go a little crispy and brown, then turn it over until the same happens on the other side. Now turn the grill down a little and cook for 5–8 minutes, depending on what tickles your fancy.

Let the meat rest for 5 minutes or so in a warm place. I promise this isn't cheffy nonsense: it really makes all the difference to the tenderness of the meat.

My perfectly crisp roasties (see page 72), and pretty peas à la franglaise (see page 78) are perfect with this. Oh, and my peperonata (see page 243) is pure perfection with lamb of any kind.

Mark's the one on the left.

Peperonata

This is one of those dishes that one just can't help *testing* while it's cooking by dipping hunks of bread into the sauce. It's dangerously more-ish. This is a really versatile dish, gorgeous hot or cold, fabulous in sandwiches, really good with jacket potatoes and cheese or stirred into scrambled eggs, and sometimes I thin it down and serve it as a soup with pesto toast. The biggest test with this dish is having anything left by the time it's ready to serve ...

SERVES 4–6
2 onions, peeled and roughly sliced
olive oil
3 large garlic cloves, peeled and finely chopped
2 red and 2 green peppers, seeded and cut into medium slices
salt
2 tbsp tomato purée
400g (14oz) can chopped tomatoes (or better still use sweet,
    flavoursome tomatoes, hard to come by on these shores)
500g (1lb 2oz) tomatoes, peeled, seeded and chopped

Sauté the onions gently in plenty of oil until translucent, then throw in the garlic and stir. Cover with the peppers, sprinkle with salt, cover the pan and leave to stew very gently for 10 minutes.

Add the tomato purée to the tomatoes, then stir into the pepper mixture. Cover and simmer gently on top of the stove, or in a moderate oven – 180°C/gas mark 4 – for 30–40 minutes, until it smells lovely and tomatoey and you can't wait to dip into it. I like to add more extra-virgin olive oil at the end; see if you do.

Jammy Duck Breasts

This dish, served with mini 'fried-in-duck-fat' potatoes, creamy collie cheese (see page 78) and green beans, is our favourite dining out/in experience. The cauliflower cheese idea might sound a bit odd with the sweet duck sauce but, believe me, the flavours all work really well together.

SERVES 2–4
4 duck breasts
sea salt and black pepper
a generous splash red wine
4 tbsp best-quality quince jam
a pinch ground cinnamon

Thoroughly dry the duck breasts and, if you have time, leave them, uncovered, in the fridge overnight. The drier the skin, the crispier you can get it.

When you're ready to cook them, score the skin with a sharp knife and rub plenty of salt into them. Lay them skin-side down in a frying pan and cook over a medium heat until they're really golden brown and the fat has reduced by at least half. Now turn them over, reduce the heat and fry on until they're cooked to your taste. Mark likes them extremely rare and we row about this one, because I think the taste and texture are sooo much better when the duck is just nicely pink.

When ready, remove and put on a warmed plate. Save that duck fat though! Potatoes fried in this are heavenly.

Whilst the duck meat rests, put the wine into the pan you cooked the duck in (fat removed!), burn off the alcohol, stirring the whole time, and now add the jam and cinnamon, and stir. Season with salt and black pepper.

With a very sharp knife, slice the duck into chunky slices and drizzle the jam over them.

Even at two years old I had a big appetite.

Big Food
for Little People

My Next Generation of Family Cooks

My offspring are total geniuses. All four of them. They are what I call my next generation of cooks, so let me introduce them to you again, in order of age, starting with the eldest.

At sixteen, Isobel (or Issy, as we all call her), my elder stepdaughter, is nearly 6 feet, willowy, leggy, beautiful, intelligent and great fun (we give each other lovely hugs). She's a true fashionista, who can (rather irritatingly) design clothes, write stories and play guitar all at the same time. She's growing into one of those über-perfect women that one loves to hate, but that one can't, because they're simply too nice and too much fun to hang out with.

At eleven, Fleur, my younger stepdaughter, is arty, hard-working, super-duper cool and trendy, and is possibly the fastest sprinter I've ever come across in my life. She's the kind of girl who decides to write, illustrate and publish a weekly periodical and sends it in the post to us. She's deceptively quiet, but if you wrong her in any way she's got that Bromley Bird in her DNA that'll tear your eyes out in a matter of seconds, and rearrange the rest of your face.

My elder girl, Maddie, is seven. Mark and I say that she saved and transformed our lives (in many different ways). She, a little like me amongst my sisters, carries the Arabic look most forcibly, with her long, dark, flowing hair and dark complexion. She's an insistent conversationalist, who will steadfastly drive home a point until you're fully paying attention. We often joke that she'd make a great politician. A fabulous dancer, she self-choreographs herself to classical music in a way that leaves you gobsmacked. Oh yes. And she loves animals. We think she'll probably end up a ballet-dancing vet.

And finally, at just two years old, Kiki Bee is the latest addition to the clan. She is quite simply nutty as a fruitcake. She has comedy bones as they say, and is mistress of pulling cross-eyed faces at all the right times. She is beautiful in a very kooky way, and thus we all call her Kooky rather than Kiki. A Virgoan through and through, she reminds many of us of her Auntie Julia, especially when she cleans and orders things into piles whilst singing at the top of her voice.

Oh yes, she also has a right hook that would make Mike Tyson proud, so if (in fifteen years' time) you ever get on the wrong side of Kiki and Fleur at the same time, you could be in a whole heap of trouble!

Needless to say, having a mum who also happens to be a Celebrity MasterChef (excuse me as I show off one more time), they all have their favourite dishes to eat, but they also all have their own little creations that they like to cook themselves. That's what I love about them: they're totally unafraid to venture into my kitchen and rustle up their own specialities. Strong, brave girls every one of them. Watch out for the Adderley girls!

Me and my lovely girls posing like rock stars!

Issy's New Year Chicken

What I loved about this meal was that Issy sprang it upon us as a total surprise. As we holidayed in lovely Cornwall, in a small cottage perched on the edge of a cliff just beside Lizard Point, Issy announced that she wanted to cook her signature chicken dish.

New Year's Eve, the wind rattling away outside, the sea crashing against the rocks, the fire stoked, and our Issy cooking us her New Year chicken! What a night! What an absolute treat being cooked for by our lovely, almost grown up (how did that happen?) Issy. I could see Mark was wide-eyed with amazement.

All of us, even wee Kiki Bee, ate, danced, sang, pulled silly faces (now a regular dining event for when we all get together) and placed party blowers up our nostrils. No wonder we collapsed at eleven o'clock — totally missing the chiming sounds of midnight!

SERVES 6
6 chicken breasts, skin on
For the marinade
a handful chopped fresh rosemary
2 garlic cloves, peeled and finely chopped
a couple of glugs olive oil
salt and black pepper

Issy put all the marinade ingredients into a bowl and really massaged the flavours into the chicken, then left them to marinate (do this for as long as you can).

Next she griddled the drained chicken breasts skin-side down until they were nice and crisp. Rather impressively, she turned them once to get a criss-cross griddle mark on the skin.

Then she popped them into a high oven (about 200°C/gas mark 6) for about 10 minutes, but tested them at around 7 minutes (her stepmother *is* a MasterChef, you know!). Her sisters, Mark and I adored every succulent mouthful. Well blooming done, Izz Biz!

Fleur — our arty party chef!

Just look at the pride on her face!

Issy in our beloved Cornwall. Aaah, take me back!

Fleur-a-Belle's Fairy Cakes

I know one isn't supposed to label children, but Fleur is 'the arty one'. Whilst Issy excels at music, fashion and writing, Maddie at dancing and Kiki Bee at abstract painting, Fleur-a-Belle (our nickname for her) has an extraordinary eye for drawing and illustrating. Because of this I always get her to make the fairy cakes. She has her own specially designated shelf in the larder, which literally groans under the weight of all the hundreds and thousands, chocolate sprinkles, half-squeezed coloured icing tubes and edible sugar flowers, all of which she has 'needed' to create her edible art. And, boy, does she create! Nobody makes fairy cakes as beautifully as my Fleur, and here's how she does it …

MAKES 12 LARGE OR 24 SMALL CAKES
125g (4½oz) butter
125g (4½oz) caster sugar
2 eggs, lightly whisked
125g (4½oz) self-raising flour, sifted
1 tsp vanilla extract, or some finely grated orange
    or lemon zest to taste
2 tbsp milk

Preheat the oven to 200°C/gas mark 6 and have ready twelve large or twenty-four small paper cake cases, put into cake or muffin tins.

In a bowl, cream the butter and sugar (by hand or with an electric beater) until light and fluffy. Whisk in the eggs slowly, alternating with spoonfuls of the sifted flour.

Fold in the remaining flour and the vanilla or orange or lemon. If the batter seems to be a bit too thick (it should drop easily off a spoon), gently stir in a little milk.

Spoon the mixture into the paper cake cases and bake for 15–20 minutes, or until nice and golden and cooked through.

Remove from the tin and allow to cool on a wire rack. Once cooled, go to town in a Fleur-a-Belle fever-like fashion, decorating them with whatever colour, glitter, balls or feathers you have lurking in your larder.

Maddie's Magic Prawns

I'm not ashamed to say that my seven-year-old daughter already knows that hearts can be won with tasty food, made with love. She already has quite an impressive repertoire: pink fairy princess cakes, carrot soup with bits (which she won't eat because of the bits), and her daddy's favourite, which she's named Maddie's magic prawns simply because she believes it is magic (and magic alone) that turns the fresh grey prawns perfectly pink, rather than the sizzling garlicky oil in which they're sautéed!

SERVES 2–4
6 tbsp olive oil
4 podgy garlic cloves, peeled and chopped
1 fresh chilli, chopped (if you like it hot)
450g (1lb) raw prawns, with or without shells
4 tbsp chopped fresh coriander
finely grated zest of ½ lemon, plus a squeeze
   of lemon (or lime) juice

In a large, non-stick frying pan, heat the oil gently and sauté the garlic (and chilli if you're using it) until it just begins to release its aroma. Be careful here, because it's at this point that this simple meal can be ruined by overcooking the garlic.

Now add the prawns and stir until the magic turns them pink. As soon as this happens, add the coriander, lemon zest and one good squeeze of lemon or lime juice.

Pour the prawns and every last bit of the juice on to the plates, alongside a green salad and plenty of crusty bread to mop up the lovely juices.

Maddie always presents this dish to her dad with the biggest, gentlest and warmest of smiles.

Kiki Bee *(The Apple of Her Daddy's Eye)*

This one is less a dish — more a fruity experiment. Mark loves to eat apples and, depending on what diet he's on, he can go from eating just six a day to eating almost thirty-two. He doesn't do anything by halves. Well, it's become a family tradition that whenever he picks up an apple and takes a bite, Kiki's hand (regardless of where she may have been standing just seconds before) immediately whips in and snatches it away from him, her daddy having lovingly broken into it and thus made it bite-able. In exchange, she will always affectionately dig around in the bottom of the fruit bowl and offer him up the last apple she nicked off him as a substitute. Equipped with his brown, rubbery, half-eaten apple, Daddy carries on with his 'snack'. As you can see, she really is the apple of her daddy's eye!

The Invisible Vegetable Soup and Icky Burnt Bread

I'm going to tell you a secret. The only vegetable my daughter Maddie will knowingly eat is sweetcorn. In the past, I've shamelessly lied to everyone about this fact, happy to let them all believe that she's a champion veggie-muncher. Why? Put simply, because I want people to think I'm the perfect mother. Oh, and because I want Maddie to eat super-healthy, scrummy food, of course.

The only strategy that really works is to make her vegetables completely invisible. So I came up with this very tasty, puréed-until-invisible vegetable soup. The first time I made it Maddie ate the lot and then, as if it was the most normal thing in the world, asked if there was any more … the Big Invisible Veg Con had worked.

I serve this with gorgeously garlicky, chargrilled ciabatta, although Maddie calls it 'icky burnt bread'. Of course you can use whatever veggies you want. Lots of veg-phobic adults love this too, by the way.

SERVES 4–6
2 leeks
4 carrots
2 medium potatoes
2 large courgettes
1 small head broccoli
½ butternut squash
2 good handfuls sweetcorn kernels
a good handful frozen peas
a knob butter (you don't have to use it, but very tasty if you do)
3 tbsp olive oil
2 litres (3½ pints) chicken stock (fresh or from concentrate)

Boring I know, but peel and chop all the veg (as necessary) to about the same size, starting with the leeks. (You won't have much to do to the peas!)

Whilst chopping the leeks, heat the butter and oil in a large, heavy-bottomed pan. Gently sauté the leeks in the oil mixture until transparent. Now add the rest of the vegetables, except the corn and sauté for 5 minutes or so.

Add the stock and bring to the boil. Turn the heat down, then simmer until soft enough to make the veg 'invisible'. Now blend until smooth in a child-friendly way and then add the corn and heat through.

'Can I Have Sausage and Mash for Pudding, Mummy?'

When Maddie has her friends over for afternoon tea, more often than not (before she's even left for school in the morning) she puts in an order for what my sometimes-irascible mother calls a 'rather silly dessert'. And there are no prizes for guessing why Maddie loves this dish so much: it's a delicious concoction of buttery caramelized bananas, covered in a melting butterscotch sauce, all served with creamy vanilla ice-cream.

I can only assume the reason my mother finds it a rather silly dessert is because of the way in which I serve it up. So long as you get your timings and your plating-up skills right, these fabulous ingredients can be assembled in such a way that it actually looks like bangers, mash and gravy. Eat your Fat Duck's heart out, Heston!

Of course, neither Maddie nor any of her friends finds this a silly dish at all. As a matter of fact, she thinks it's brilliant. I love eavesdropping from the hall as she launches into a detailed and earnest explanation for her friends. Bear in mind, Maddie never, ever pauses for breath. And I mean never.

'You know I've got a MasterChef mummy? Well, that's because she's so clever … [I usually start blubbing at this point.] That's right. She's so clever that she makes magic sausages out of camamillized bananas, and look, look … see the mashed potatoes? She magicks them out of vanilla ice-cream and — the gravy … [At this point she is usually on tiptoe — the end of her description bringing her ever closer to taking her first bite!] The gravy … look at the gravy … it's not really gravy … it's actually BUTTERSPLOTCH SAUCE!' At this point there are usually great gasps of appreciation from her schoolfriends (mixed with a few stomach rumbles) before, finally, Maddie allows them to dive in.

Bangers, Mash and Gravy *(for Dessert)*

I promise you, this bizarre concoction is well worth making in order to witness those expectant little faces melting into ear-to-ear smiles as they tuck in, realizing that when they get home they can justifiably say to their own parents that they've already had dinner over at Maddie's. 'What did you have?' their parents will ask. 'Bangers, mash and gravy,' they'll reply loudly. 'For dessert,' they'll mutter just out of earshot …

SERVES 4
For the 'sausages'
about 40g (1½oz) butter
3 tbsp sugar (I use light brown)
4 ripe but firm bananas, peeled
For the 'gravy'
85g (3oz) soft brown sugar
125ml (4 fl. oz) double cream
85g (3oz) butter
For the 'mash'
your favourite vanilla, or maybe banana, ice-cream

Start by melting the butter and sugar for the 'sausages' in a heavy frying pan. Add the whole bananas and leave over a gentle heat to caramelize on all sides. Remove from the pan with a slotted spoon.

For the 'gravy', put the sugar, cream and butter in a pan over a medium heat and keep stirring (so pleasurable) until the sugar dissolves. Now simmer for 2–3 minutes. Turn off the heat and cover to keep warm.

Pile the ice-cream 'mash' into the middle of each serving plate. Stand the bananas on end all round it, then pour the brown sugar 'gravy' over the top and round the edge of the plate. Now beam at your little darlings as you serve … bangers, mash and gravy for dessert.

Maddie in sweet-bangers-and-mash heaven.

Aahhh, Pancakes!

As a child, I had a prayer that I would mutter to myself: 'God please, please let there be pancakes tomorrow and I will be the best kid ever. I will go to bed at bedtime without being asked, I will eat all my spinach (even though it's disgusting) and I will empty the dishwasher every day. Amen.' You see, our mum didn't make just any old pancakes: she made the best pancakes in the world.

She always used the same utterly divine French recipe. I would know that my prayers had been answered on the days Mum did the highly unusual thing of slipping a couple of whole eggs, shells and all, on to the scale pan. This was the basis of her rather special recipe, as whatever the eggs (with shell) weighed, Mum would match with an equal amount of flour, sugar and (wait for it) butter. Then came her twist: she would add a large spoonful of brandy: 'That's to make them lacy.' This was always said with resounding authority, as I merely gazed up at her opening the bottle, in wonder at her pure genius. Actually, now I think of it, I seem to remember 'brandy making things lacy' being a common 'top tip' in our kitchen …

My mother unfortunately would only make these beauties half a dozen or so times a year, which in those days I thought was (a) tantamount to neglect and (b) very inconsiderate of God, given how much I prayed to him. Indeed, I remember promising over and over to myself, 'When I have children I'm going to make them pancakes every day!'

And, although I haven't quite kept that particular promise, for my sins I do make them every weekend. As a consequence I have now developed a real understanding of why my mother was so reluctant to cook them day in, day out all those years ago. It takes blooming hours of frying and flipping to make enough of them to satisfy my two daughters, two stepdaughters, two nephews (Zak and Finlay) and a forever skulking husband (who loves to nick them and spread Nutella on them). So, for those days when I simply don't have the time, I've devised my very own *français* recipe for pancakes, which are just as delicious as my mum's but, more importantly, much, much more filling. Two each usually keeps 'em quiet!

Apple Pancakes

I first tried something similar to these delicious apple pancakes in Germany when I was six years old. It's taken me years of trial and error to get a recipe that lives up to my childhood memories of them …

SERVES 4–6
175g (6oz) plain flour
3 tsp ground cinnamon
2 large eggs
200ml (7 fl. oz) milk mixed with 100ml (3½ fl. oz) water
1 tbsp Calvados (optional, if cooking for kids)
115g (4oz) unsalted butter, melted, plus extra for frying
115g (4oz) caster sugar
4 small sweet apples, peeled, cored and grated
For the vanilla cream
300ml (½ pint) double cream, whipped with 1 tsp vanilla extract

Sift the flour and cinnamon into a bowl. Make a hollow in the centre and break the eggs into it, then add the milk and water, the Calvados (if using) and melted butter. Whisk into the flour a little at a time, then whisk in the sugar. Once the mixture is all lovely and smooth, stir in the grated apples (I always get my little ones to grate them).

Melt enough extra butter to coat the bottom and sides of a small, heavy frying pan. Put a ladleful of the batter into the hot pan and swirl it around so that it totally covers the base. Cook until the edges begin to turn nicely golden, crisp and 'lacy', then flip over and cook until the other side is golden too. Each pancake will want its own little knob of butter melted in the pan for frying.

Serve with whipped vanilla cream for dessert, or yogurt if you're having them for breakfast (though I have to admit I always have cream).

Desserts: The Perfect End
to a Perfect Meal

The Most Foul-mouthed Lemon Soufflé in the World

I've learned all my favourite swear words from my mother. This is mainly due to the fact that every now and then something very scary happens to her in the kitchen.

Now don't get me wrong — for the most part my mum is a real lady.

Sometimes when I was little my sisters and I would arrive home from school, only to be stopped in our tracks at the garden gate as we were met by our mother's blasphemous shouts of frustration emanating from a rattling letterbox. It was as though the front door itself were having a rant.

As we heard a range of F-words, S-words, B-words — and some swear words at which we could only marvel — we would look at each other and in unison mouth rather nervously, 'She's making dessert!' We would tentatively turn the key, mindful the whole time that, as the door edged open, we might be hit by sweet sticky shrapnel or even an entire recipe book.

So how strange it is to acknowledge that one of the desserts that was responsible for so many demonic episodes in my mother's life is a pudding so light, gentle, serene and seductive in its lemony loveliness that everyone who tasted it could be forgiven for thinking it was actually made by an angel. Once we had stepped into the kitchen, dumped our schoolbags and eaten our main course, this truly magical creation (a dish of sublime citrus calm-after-the-storm-ness) would emerge straight from the blaspheming hands of our now exhausted-looking mother.

So if you're hoping to increase the money in your swear-box, read on. I've added my mother's more colourful explosions to the recipe, in such a way that they can be re-enacted alongside those particularly complex moments.

By the way, Mum (who lives next door) has just walked in and read this. She wants me to make it very clear that the only reason she had any trouble in the kitchen was because of 'the continuous bloody racket she had to put up with in the madhouse that was our home!'

DESSERTS: THE PERFECT END TO A PERFECT MEAL

@&!!@** Lemon Soufflé!

Whenever Mum made this lemon soufflé there was usually some 'posh' reason for it. So, the biscuit of choice would be the *trés* posh *langue du chat*. With their buttery taste and baked-dry texture, they went perfectly with the cloud-like softness of the soufflé. Why they are called 'tongue of the cat' is anybody's guess.

SERVES 6–8
4 medium eggs
225g (8oz) caster sugar
finely grated zest and juice of 3 lemons ['Good grief –
    it's totally %@!!!!** gone in my eye!']
300ml (½ pint) double cream, plus extra to whip for decoration
10g (¼oz) powdered gelatine, soaked in 5 tsp cold water; do not
    stir ['Why do I always @*:!!!!! forget the amount of water?']
85g (3oz) flaked almonds, toasted and finely chopped

Before you start, you need a large basin of iced water in which to cool and set the soufflé.

Separate the eggs. Put the yolks in a large bowl with the sugar, lemon zest and juice, and beat together until very thick and creamy.

Whip the cream until the ribbon stage; do *not* over-whip! ['Easier @**% said than **** done!']

Whip the egg whites by hand until just standing in peaks; do not allow them to become too stiff. [' *@.**!! stiff to one person isn't *!!!!??@ stiff for someone else!']

Stir the gelatine into the cream and then stir into the egg-yolk mixture.

Lightly fold in the egg whites with a palette knife until well mixed.

Put the bowl of mixture into the bowl of iced water and then into the fridge. Give it a stir every 20 minutes or so, reaching well down to the bottom, until you feel it thickening. If you don't mix well at this stage ['@!x@!!!!!'], you will end up with a lemon jelly at the bottom of the bowl and a lemon foam on top. ['*@**!!!']

Pour into the bowl of your choice and, just before serving, decorate with whipped cream (optional) and browned almonds (which are sooooo easy to burn ['@@!!****']).

And there you have possibly the most foul-mouthed lemon soufflé in the world!

Betty's Pear Tart with Armagnac *(Lots!)*

Dad really loves this tart and he would walk around with a big grin on his face when he knew Mum had one planned. He's a sucker for pears anyway, and the orange and almond give an exotic Middle Eastern flavour to this dessert. With his passion for pears and Mum's passion for Armagnac, this dessert is a heavenly fusion of parental preferences.

SERVES 4–6

For the almond pastry
225g (8oz) plain flour
115g (4oz) caster sugar
115g (4oz) butter, softened
3 egg yolks
1–2 drops almond essence
115g (4oz) ground almonds

For the filling
2–3 ripe dessert pears, peeled, cored and quartered
1 tbsp caster sugar
finely grated zest and juice of ½ orange
2 tbsp Armagnac

To finish
1 egg white, lightly whipped
caster sugar

Sift the flour into a bowl, make a well in the centre and put in the sugar, butter, egg yolks and almond essence. Sprinkle the ground almonds over the mixture. With the fingers of one hand work the ingredients to a firm paste. Place in a polythene bag and refrigerate for about an hour.

Now prepare the filling. Sprinkle the pears with the sugar, orange zest and juice and the Armagnac. Cover and leave for 30 minutes.

Preheat the oven to 190°C/gas mark 5 and have ready a 20cm (8in) flan ring.

Roll out a good third of the pastry to the diameter of the flan ring. Stamp out a 6cm (2½in) circle from the middle – the piece with the hole will be the top of the tart – and put the cut-out circle with the rest of the pastry. Roll this out and use it to line the base and sides of the flan ring.

Drain the pears and reserve the juice. Fill the tart with the pears and cover with the pastry top. Press and trim around the edge. Bake for 35–40 minutes.

About 5 minutes before the tart is cooked, remove it from the oven and brush it with the slightly broken egg white, then dust quickly with caster sugar. Return to the oven to frost the top. Serve hot or cold with whipped cream.

Cousin Elias's Easy-peasy Carrot Cake

I would love to tell you that this gorgeous (and astonishingly easy) carrot cake recipe is one of my teenage creations, but unfortunately I cannot. It's actually my cousin Elias's and he's famous in the family for it. In fact, I doubt there's been a family party, wedding, funeral or christening in the past thirty years without this delicious cake taking pride of place on the dessert table. So you can rest assured this recipe has been well and truly tested!

MAKES A 20CM (8IN) CAKE
115g (4oz) butter, melted
3 eggs, beaten
5 heaped tbsp natural yogurt
225g (8oz) carrots, peeled and grated
175g (6oz) ground almonds
115g (4oz) soft light brown sugar
115g (4oz) shelled walnuts, chopped
55g (2oz) desiccated coconut
115g (4oz) stoned dates, chopped
1 tsp ground cinnamon
½ tsp freshly grated nutmeg
1 tsp baking powder

Preheat the oven to 170°C/gas mark 3. Grease a 20cm (8in) round cake tin and line it with lightly oiled greaseproof paper.

Mix together the melted butter and beaten eggs. You're not going to believe this, but you've already nearly made this cake. Add the yogurt, then the carrots and all the remaining dry ingredients. Mix well.

Pour the mixture into the prepared cake tin and bake for approximately 1 hour. Leave to cool in the tin, then turn out on to a wire rack to become completely cold.

Rosewater and Pistachio Ice-cream

I made this exotic ice-cream for the *MasterChef* final and both the judges literally swooned (in fact Gregg said he wanted to live next door to me!). When I'm feeling really, really naughty, I serve it with baklava (see page 266), but to try to lessen my evil deed I make the baklava very, very small.

SERVES 4–6
150ml (5 fl. oz) full-fat milk
150ml (5 fl. oz) double cream
55g (2oz) shelled ground pistachio nuts
½ tsp very finely ground cardamom seeds
   (I use a pestle and mortar)
2 egg yolks
85g (3oz) caster sugar
2 tbsp rosewater
a drop red food colouring to give a rosy glow
   (optional, but it does look so pretty with it)
rose petals to decorate (optional)

Pour the milk, cream, nuts and cardamom into a saucepan. Bring to the boil, then put to one side. In a mixing bowl beat the egg yolks and sugar until they're pale, then beat in the boiled cream and milk. Now put it all back into the saucepan and stir constantly over a really low heat, until it's the consistency of custard, but *do not* allow it to boil — trust me, there will be a disaster! Now add the rosewater and food colouring, put it all into your ice-cream-maker and churn till thick and creamy. If you don't have an ice-cream-maker, put the mixture in a plastic container in the freezer, stirring every now and again to break up the ice crystals. Scatter some rose petals on the top to serve.

Baklava *(Sent Direct from Heaven)*

I must warn you that these delightful delicacies are an extremely expensive indulgence that should probably be allowed out only once a year. Feel free to experiment a bit with the flower waters: I know that some (strange) people aren't keen on their perfume, whilst others can't get enough.

MAKES 20–25 PASTRIES

For the filling
350g (12oz) shelled pistachio nuts, finely chopped
2 tbsp caster sugar
1 tbsp rosewater
1 tsp ground cardamom (my nephew Zak has insisted
  on 'optional', as he hates cardamom)

For the syrup
300ml (½ pint) water
450g (1lb) granulated sugar
1 tbsp lemon juice
1 tbsp each rosewater and orange-flower water

For the pastry
450g (1lb) packet fresh filo pastry
250g (9oz) unsalted butter, melted

Mix the filling ingredients together in a bowl, cover, and set aside. Preheat the oven to 180°C/gas mark 4, and butter a 30 x 28cm (12 x 11in) baking tray.

Next, make the syrup to allow time for it to cool. Bring the water, sugar and lemon juice to the boil in a medium saucepan. Do not stir, but keep it at a bubble for about 4–5 minutes. Add the heady flower waters and set to one side to cool until those naughty pastries are ready to be bathed in it.

Unwrap the pastry and keep it under a damp towel. This is really important, because it's incredible how quickly the pastry can dry out. Lay one sheet in the tray and brush it with butter (though if I'm honest I spread it with my hands, as it's less likely to tear). Repeat this until you've used half the packet and don't press down on the pastry so that it can puff up a bit. Time to scatter the twinkling sugared pistachio mixture all over the pastry. Repeat the buttering and layering of the remaining pastry until all used up.

With a sharp knife, cut a diamond pattern all the way through, though I usually just cut it into squares. Bake for 20 minutes, then increase the temperature to 220°C/gas mark 7 and cook for 10–15 minutes until puffed and golden.

Pour the syrup on slowly, as you may find you don't need it all. Baklava is *supposed* to be eaten cold but Zak and I have never been able to wait that long!

A Refreshingly Liquid Pit-stop

These two fabulous beverages are a perfect accompaniment to the baklava and/or the rosewater and pistachio ice-cream (see pages 266 and 264). I wouldn't advise you to have both, but each certainly completes a meal in its own way. Also, you can pretty much divide the world into those who prefer mint tea and those who require Turkish coffee … though my husband, rather typically, likes them both. Beverages have always proved to be something of a weakness in his life!

Mint Tea

When I was a child I used to love going into downtown Amman with my mum because, whatever shop or stall we went to, we would be served with tiny, brightly coloured glasses of super-sweet mint tea. Poured out of beautiful silver teapots from an ever-increasing height, the bubbling sound of it collecting in your small, finely wrought glass makes your mouth water. The sweet aromatic taste of this drink is an absolute winner. I just don't understand why more people don't drink it in the UK! All my four girls devour it whenever we are in Morocco or Jordan.

Put a large bunch of washed mint into a warmed teapot and, if you like, a couple of teaspoons of green tea. Pour boiling water over and leave to stand for 5 minutes or so. We each add our own sugar to taste, but, if everyone's in agreement, you can add it to the pot with the mint. Serve in small glasses. A fantastic digestive and nerve calmer — oh, and really good for morning sickness too!

Turkish Coffee

This is one of my dad's specialities; in fact, he doesn't really let anyone else make it. The aroma as he boils it up on the stove evokes such wonderful memories that I'm always very happy to lie back and inhale whilst letting him get on with it. Again, it is surprisingly sweet in taste, and remarkably thick. I remember Mark first trying it. Even he, a seasoned drinker of great repute, couldn't disguise the slightly dry effect it had on his throat. That said, he found it (surprise, surprise) strangely addictive.

PER PERSON
1 Arabic coffee cup (approx. 55ml (2 fl. oz)) water
1 level tsp sugar (for medium-sweet)
1 green cardamom pod, lightly crushed
1 heaped tsp very dark, finely ground coffee
  (we use half Kenyan, half mocha)

Put the water into a Turkish coffee pot or a small saucepan. Add the sugar and cardamom, then stir in the coffee. Bring to the boil, remove from the heat until the coffee dies down, then scoop off some of the foam and put into the first cup. Then repeat, bringing it back to the boil three times in all, each time spooning some foam into the cups. (Dad is very particular about this: 'You boil it once, you boil it again, and then once more.') Pour very slowly into the tiny cups.

   If you really love cardamom, put some in the coffee jar as well!

Weekend Family Get-together

Friday evenings are like controlled explosions in my house, almost without exception. As soon as the long arm hits six, all hell breaks loose.

Generally my sister Julia is the first to arrive, exhausted from a week's filming, having had to endure some incredibly tiny period costume and now desperate for a break from hotel food. No sooner does her luggage hit the already chaotic kitchen floor than my daughter Maddie is clinging to her neck, before her magical auntie produces a characteristic selection of foodie delights: plump, sticky Iranian dates and her home-made avocado dip, both gloriously healthy and thankfully delicious too.

Before there's even time to trade our latest gossip, hot on her heels comes Mark with my stepdaughters Issy and Fleur. They're not only hungry but also bursting at the seams with girly chat.

So, generally, at just 6.15, luggage-wise the kitchen resembles Heathrow's Terminal 5 rather than the beating heart and soul of a family home. The volume is always earsplitting, the peals of laughter almost deafening; and yet, beneath it all, I can always just about make out the very different moans, groans and creaks of everyone's stomachs, desperately anticipating the dinner (or dinners) I'm about to make.

Whilst Mark is hoping for a sinfully creamy lasagne, Issy and Fleur are always wishing for a heavenly, roasted garlic-butter chicken with tiny crisp roast potatoes; and when my nephew Zak arrives, if there's no sign of his favourite spicy meatballs he immediately dials the kebab shop or Nando's. And finally, there is always the challenge of concocting something delicious for Julia.

It therefore comes as a massive relief that, in all the musical mayhem of cooking up to six very different main courses for eight larger-than-life personalities, I know there is at least one culinary consensus of opinion in my house. Thankfully everyone (and I mean everyone) adores my raspberry hazelnut meringues. Though, generally, at the point they're all tucking into these tasty morsels, I'm tucking into *my* favourite dessert: vodka and slimline tonic …

Raspberry Hazelnut Meringue

This really is quite easy to make and people will fall in love with you for it. It's a gorgeously crisp-but-chewy, dangerously sweet hazelnut meringue, smothered in clouds of vanilla cream, topped with velvety, crimson-red raspberries, finished with a flourish of snowy icing sugar. Mmmmmmeringue heaven!

SERVES 6
350g (12oz) shelled hazelnuts
6 egg whites
375g (13oz) caster sugar
5–6 drops vanilla extract
¾ tsp raspberry vinegar
600ml (1 pint) double cream
2 tbsp Frangelico, or other hazelnut liqueur
   (omit if kids are eating), plus a cook's glug
500g (1lb 2oz) fresh raspberries
icing sugar

Preheat the oven to 150°C/gas mark 2 and line a Swiss roll tin with buttered baking parchment.

Dry-toast the hazelnuts under the grill until they're almost burning. When cool, finely chop the nuts. No nibbling!

Whisk the egg whites until stiff. Add 1 tbsp of the sugar and whisk for 1 minute. Then gradually add the remaining sugar, 1 tbsp at a time, and continue whisking until the mixture turns glossy and stands in obedient peaks.

Whisk in the vanilla extract and raspberry vinegar (the vinegar gives the gorgeous chewy texture, but amazingly *no* vinegary taste; you only get the flavour of raspberries). Now carefully fold in the toasted nuts.

Spoon the mixture on to the baking parchment in the Swiss roll tin about 2.5cm (1in) thick all over.

Bake for 40–50 minutes. The top of the meringue should be crisp, the inside like a gooey marshmallow. Whilst still in the baking tray, using a heart-shaped cutter, cut out an even number of shapes.

Whip the cream until lusciously thick, but be careful not to overdo it or it will curdle. Gently stir in the Frangelico or other liqueur (this is the time for your glug). Pile a couple of tablespoons of cream on to half the heart shapes, then place your raspberries gently on the cream. Place the second heart on top and dust with icing sugar.

The Great British Crumble ... the Arabic Way

My fella has a serious addiction ... to raisins, sultanas, dates, apricots. In fact, any dried fruit that tries to reside in our kitchen has a very short life-expectancy. Wherever I hide them for Maddie's packed lunches, Mark seeks them out and destroys them *all* in a matter of seconds.

Mark also needs his oats every day ... porridge oats, of course! I kept these two facts firmly in my mind whilst dreaming up this birthday dessert for him: a buttery, cinnamon-flavoured apple, sultana and pine-nut oaty crumble. He loved every morsel, and I say *every* morsel because he wouldn't let anyone else get a look in ... well, it *was* his birthday!

SERVES 6
For the filling
55g (2oz) butter
1.3kg (3lb) apples (I use Coxes, but feel free to
    use whatever you fancy), peeled and quartered
85g (3oz) sultanas
For the crumble
250g (9oz) oats
115g (4oz) pine nuts
140g (5oz) butter, cut into cubes
2 heaped tsp cinnamon
85g (3oz) dark brown sugar
1–2 tbsp caster sugar

Pre-heat the oven to 180°C/gas mark 4. Butter a 30 x 20cm (12 x 8in) gratin dish.

To make the filling, melt the butter in a large frying pan and, once it starts to bubble, throw in the apples. Cook them on a medium heat for a couple of minutes, then reduce the heat and cook for a couple more minutes until they're softened but not cooked through. Stir in the sultanas and then pour the fruits into your dish.

Now make the crumble. Put all the ingredients (apart from the caster sugar) in a lovely big bowl and rub the butter in until it's all thoroughly mixed. Scatter the crumble over the waiting apples, dot with more butter then sprinkle the caster sugar all over, until the crumble twinkles. Bake for 30–40 minutes. Mark is weird and likes his crumble really cold with cream. I, on the other hand, love mine hot with ice-cream!

Mouhallabieh *(Rose-scented Rice Pudding)*

I love making this dessert for my dad, as it is the all-time favourite comfort food from his childhood. It requires a serious amount of stirring, which is what makes it a real labour of love, but it's far more 'love' than 'labour' for me!

SERVES 4–6
115g (4oz) finely ground rice
125ml (4 fl. oz) warm water
1.2 litres (2 pints) full-fat milk
85g (3oz) caster sugar
1 tbsp each orange-flower water and rosewater
55g (2oz) shelled pistachios, whole or chopped
6 stoned dates, chopped

Put the rice and water in a heavy-bottomed pan and heat on a medium heat. Whisking continuously, add the milk and sugar. Now bring it up to the boil and, still stirring, boil for a couple of minutes. Reduce the heat and carry on stirring continuously until the rice has thickened. This takes about 15 minutes, but it's such a soothing 15 minutes you won't resent the time spent at the stove!

Now add those wonderful flower waters and give it all a few more stirs for luck. Remove from the heat and, pretty sharpish (it starts to set really quickly), pour into individual bowls. Sprinkle with the chopped or whole pistachios and dates.

Kunafeh *(Shredded Pastry Filled with Soft Cheese and Syrup)*

This is Dina and Dad's favourite Middle Eastern dessert. It's a speciality of Damascus, where, rather conveniently, Dina's ex-boyfriend's mother was from, so we learned straight from the horse's mouth. At its simplest, you'll always know when you're being served kunafeh, because the pastry looks a little like Shredded Wheat.

This dessert is a very appropriate response to a famous Syrian saying: 'There is an empty place in my stomach that only sweets can fill.'

SERVES 4–6

For the syrup
350ml (12 fl. oz) water
350g (12oz) caster sugar
juice of ½ lemon
2 tbsp rosewater

For the pastry base
400g (14oz) kunafeh pastry
200g (7oz) unsalted butter, melted (throw
    away the milk solids left at the bottom)

For the filling
350g (12oz) mizithra cheese or ricotta
1 tbsp caster sugar
1 tbsp rosewater
finely grated zest of 1 unwaxed lemon

Preheat the oven to 180°C/gas mark 4. Grease a shallow ovenproof dish.

First make the syrup, following the syrup instructions for baklava (page 266). Put it aside to cool.

Now put the pastry in a bowl and pull apart the strands, being careful not to break them. Pour the clarified butter over the pastry, gently making sure every strand is coated in butter.

Put all the filling ingredients in another bowl and mix them thoroughly.

Put half the pastry mixture into the bottom of the greased dish, press it down and spoon the cheese filling evenly over it. Now cover it with the rest of the pastry, pop it into the oven and bake until it's golden: about 30–45 minutes.

As soon as you take it out, pour on the syrup (or you can serve it on the side). When it's cold, cut into squares or, if you're a clever dick, diamonds!

Arabic-y Trifle

It's hilarious: my thoroughly Arabic dad, for whom I invented this 'Arabic' trifle (because he adores trifle), won't flaming well touch it, saying, 'Why muck about with something that doesn't need it, *Nadyah*!' Well I, and everyone else who's tried it, think that my brave leap of faith has paid off. All in all, a fabulous twist on an old favourite. Did you get that, Dad? I said '*twist* on an *old* favourite'!

SERVES 4–6
200g (7oz) organic soft-dried apricots, soaked in boiling
    water for an hour
175g (6oz) packet trifle sponges
medium sherry, to taste
425ml (¾ pint) double cream
a handful shelled whole pistachios
For the custard
1 vanilla pod
600ml (1 pint) full-fat milk
3 cardamom pods, lightly crushed
5 egg yolks
1 ½ tbsp caster sugar
a handful slivered almonds

For the custard, with a sharp knife open up the vanilla pod and scrape out the sticky seeds. Now throw the seeds and pod into a small saucepan with the milk and cardamom, and heat gently to allow the spices to give out their flavour fully.

Whisk the egg yolks and sugar in a bowl. Take the vanilla pod out of the milk and sieve the milk slowly over the egg mixture, stirring constantly. Pour back into the saucepan (I know it's a bit of a palaver, but the taste is worth it) and on a really slow heat keep stirring for 10–15 minutes until it has the consistency of thick double cream. Patience is a real virtue whilst making custard!

Now, toast the almonds. You might need more than you think, because if you're anything like me, no matter how careful I am, I always burn the first lot!

Put half the apricots in the bottom of your loveliest glass bowl. Now cover with some of the sponges and trickle the sherry all over them. Cover with the cardamom-infused custard. Repeat the whole delicious process.

Whip the cream, pile it on top of the trifle, then decorate with toasted almonds and pistachios.

Tropical Treacle Tart

A dream come true for anyone with a sweet tooth! You can use shop-bought pastry, but if you fancy spending a little more time in the kitchen, the pastry recipe below is foolproof.

SERVES 8
For the shortcrust pastry
225g (8oz) plain flour (don't use flour that has been
   hanging about for ages, as this can ruin the pastry)
a pinch fine salt
55g (2oz) lard
55g (2oz) butter, plus extra for greasing
1–2 tbsp chilled water
For the treacle filling
7 tbsp golden syrup
115g (4oz) desiccated coconut, toasted
finely grated zest of 1 lime, plus juice of ½ lime
To serve
whipped vanilla double cream or ice-cream

Put the flour and salt in a sieve and, holding it as high as possible, sift it into a roomy bowl. Cut the fat into small cubes and drop into the bowl. With a knife, cut the butter into the flour. Next, using the very tips of your fingers, rub the butter into the flour until you get a breadcrumb look. Sprinkle a little of the water in and, with a knife, start bringing the mixture together, then finally, using your hands, gently bring it all into a ball. Pop into a bag and chill for 30 minutes. Leave this bit out at your peril.

Butter a 20cm (8in) fluted tart tin, then roll the pastry out to a circle large enough to fit the base and sides of your tin. Put it into the tin and pop it back in the fridge for 30 minutes. Put any trimmings to one side, covered.

Preheat the oven to 190°C/gas mark 5.

Now make the filling. With a hot spoon (to help the syrup slide off) measure the syrup into a bowl and add the toasted coconut, lime zest and juice. Give it all a really good stir. Now pour it into the pastry-lined tin. Roll out the pastry trimmings, cut them into long strips and make a criss-cross pattern across the filling of the tart — not easy. I often make a right royal mess of it, but it's necessary to keep the syrup from overflowing the sides of the tart. Use cold water to make the strips stick to the pastry sides.

Bake for about 30–35 minutes. Serve warm with lots of wicked whipped vanilla cream and/or ice-cream.

Best Job in the World?
Not on Your Nelly!

After I'd won *Celebrity MasterChef* in 2007, Mark came up with the fabulous idea for *Eating in the Sun*, made by our production company and presented by me. Genius, eh?

The terrifying premise of the show is that a famous chef from the UK challenges me to travel to the country where they once had their most memorable holiday meal and cook for them there. I'd get just one chance to practise cooking each course before the big day. I'd travel around sourcing the ingredients, then when the day arrived, so would the chef, and I would *for the first time* discover who I was cooking for. It was utterly terrifying.

Whilst filming the first episode, I found myself in southern Italy (the Sassi to be exact), challenged to make the perfect ricotta cheesecake. Easy-peasy, I thought. I had a spring in my step, a twinkle in my eye — *this* was going to be a doddle. Oh, I couldn't have been more mistaken!

Cut to … six the following morning, and I'm standing in the middle of a field with the director — who is also, rather bravely (and absurdly), my husband Mark — telling me to milk a very frisky-looking sheep. Why, you ask? Well, given that he is a self-confessed non-foodie and yet takes himself seriously as a programme-maker, he wanted to go back to the very *first* step involved in making ricotta cheese — milking a flaming sheep! To any other director I would have given short shrift but, with an entire farm waiting for the Englishwoman to arrive, I simply had to do as I was told …

Now, stroking a cat terrifies me, so you can imagine how frightened I was when it came to milking a sheep. The next hour was a total blur but, according to the crew, I sat on a strange man's lap, milked said sheep, got covered in sheep poo, fell off said lap, stirred and stirred and stirred, and … with the leftover whey from making some pecorino cheese, I eventually made my own ricotta.

I was so proud … until I heard Mark talking with the locals about the following day's shoot. His exact words were, 'I think that went really well. Tomorrow, can we try the same, only with buffalo mozzarella …?'

Ricotta Cheesecake

I have to say, in the end the cheesecake was sublime. Obviously the ricotta was heavenly, and I flavoured it with lemons picked from the roadside, and the best limoncello I've ever tasted. Even though Mark begged me, I didn't offer him even the teeniest, tiniest taste.

SERVES 6–8

For the ricotta mixture
900g (2lb) fresh ricotta cheese
175g (6oz) granulated sugar, plus extra for finishing
a good big glug limoncello
3 eggs
finely grated zest of 1 lemon

For the pastry
350g (12oz) plain flour
150g (5½oz) butter, cut into cubes
150g (5½oz) granulated sugar
1 whole egg, plus 1–2 extra egg yolks, if necessary
finely grated zest of 1 lemon

To make the filling, put the ricotta and sugar into a blender, if you have one. If not, prepare for achey arms. Blend on low until the sugar is nicely combined, then slosh in the limoncello and mix in. Add the eggs one at a time, waiting for each one to be thoroughly mixed in before adding the next. On a slow speed this should take a good 2 minutes, no less. Now stir in the lemon zest.

For the pastry, put the flour into a bowl and add the cubes of butter. Rub together until the mixture resembles breadcrumbs. Add the sugar and the whole egg and mix together. To get the right shortbread-like texture, you might need to add an egg yolk or maybe two. Mix in the lemon zest.

Preheat the oven to 180°C/gas mark 4, and lightly butter and flour a 25cm (10in) round pie tin.

Roll the pastry out on a lightly floured surface to about 3mm (⅛in) thick. Put it into the prepared tin. Save any spare pieces to make a lattice.

Pour in the gorgeously creamy ricotta mixture and cover with a pastry lattice, then sprinkle with granulated sugar and bake for 40–45 minutes. It should really puff up high when it's ready, but don't be disappointed like I was when you take it out of the oven and it sinks back down.

The Italians were horrified when I ate this warm, insisting it should be eaten the next day. Sorry, I'm not blessed with Mediterranean patience!

Index

The cast and crew that made this book happen

For the past nine months or so, my life has resembled a culinary earthquake. So, for all those people who have been caught up in the emotion, trauma and airborne ingredients that have surrounded the pulling together of this book, a huge apology for the expletives, and an even bigger apology for the mess.

Mark Adderley — my gorgeous husband, who gave me the courage to pull this book off and the loan of his brilliant brain whenever I needed it. Not to mention the many beautiful photos of our lives together that are peppered throughout the book. As my mum says, 'Is there nothing the bugger can't do?' My hero, my friend and a dream dad to our beautiful girls. 'Egg and … sandwich, anyone?'

Roberta/Bobbie/Betty Sawalha — my marvellous mum, whose patience and enthusiasm have been invaluable. She's given me hours of practical help. While I type with two fingers, she types a hundred words a minute, so I'll leave the maths to you! Most importantly, she has passed on to me her passion for food and cooking, which has not only brought me great joy, but also produced this book. Oh yes, and she makes a mean 'end-of-the-day' gin and tonic too!

Nadim Joakim Sawalha — a true patriarch, whose magical talent for storytelling and unique sense of humour have rung in my ears as I've written this book. His bravery in making a go of it here in Britain gave me the gift of two cultures to pick and choose from, and pick and choose I did. Thank God this wise and wonderful man is my dad and thank God for his bonkers, totally off-the-wall family, otherwise what on earth would I have written about?

Julia Sawalha — my little sister and best friend. Her sense of humour makes me glad to be alive. Her courage astounds me. Her wisdom nourishes me. And only she knows what I mean when I say, 'I was about seven when …'

Dina Sawalha — my big sister, and the best cook I know. I miss you and that will never change. x

Zak, Finlay, Issy, Fleur, Maddie and Kiki Bee — the precious children in my life who will always let me know when something is 'yuk' or 'tastes like sick'!

Rachel Packer — a true healer and a true friend. How much harder life would have been without you. x

Julia (not my sister!) — the best trainer in the world, not only because she has succeeded where many others have failed (yes, I NOW LOVE EXERCISE!), but also because she happily joins me in endless chat about food and wine as we run, jump and lunge together! Top bird!

Kaye Adams — the most brilliant bird I have ever 'hung loose' with. I love you. Always have. x

Julie Salih — a great woman and a great cheesecake-maker. If only we could get the recipe!

Nigel Slater — after my mother, my food hero. You will never know how completely you have transformed my and my family's life.

Rosemary Scoular — my agent, who manages to have balls of steel and yet still be lovely!

Becky Jones — my editor. Crikey, how can someone so young be so bloomin' cool, calm, collected and clever?

Doug Young — a man of great courage and vision who, amazingly, allowed me to keep *Stuffed Vine Leaves Saved My Life* as the title of this book when others dared to suggest horrors like *Nadia's Nibbles* and *Noshing with Nads*. God forbid!

Steve Lee — thank you for seeing what I knew I wanted to see, but could never describe!

Clare Greenstreet — for your fabulous cooking!

Smith & Gilmour — for bringing great style to the table, and to Lily for her beautiful potato prints!

Kirsty Jones (and her mum) — you both know what you did with *that* book. Sshhh, our secret.